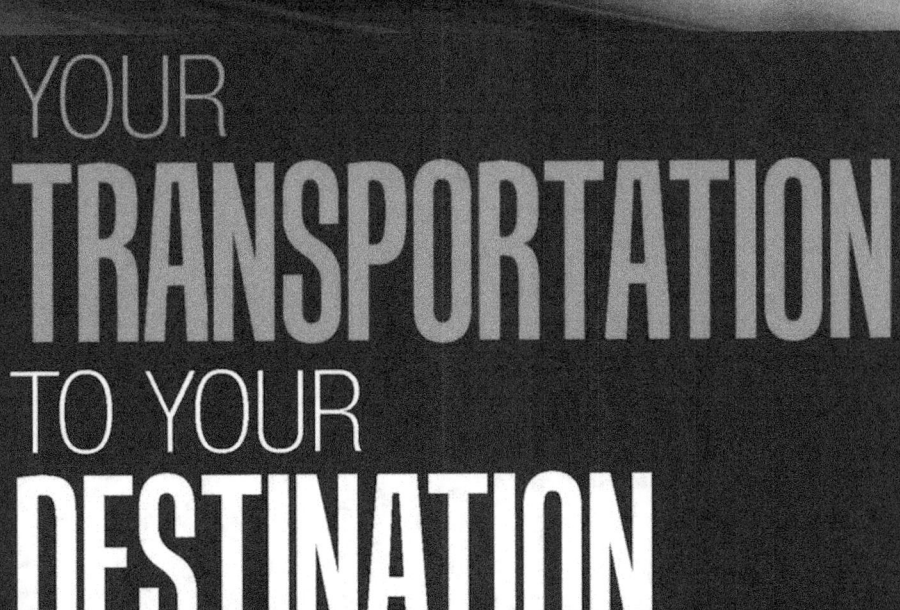

Miss Marcia P Mattis

YOUR TRANSPORTATION TO YOUR DESTINATION

Your Life's Journey

Copyright @2021 by Marcia Mattis

All rights reserved. No part of this book may be reproduced in any form or by any electronic or mechanical means, including information storage and retrieval systems, without permission in writing from the publisher, except by reviewers, who may quote brief passages in a review.

This publication contains the opinions and ideas of its author. It is intended to provide helpful and informative material on the subjects addressed in the publication. The author and publisher specifically disclaim all responsibility for any liability, loss or risk, personal or otherwise, which is incurred as a consequence, directly or indirectly, of the use and application of any of the contents of this book.

WORKBOOK PRESS LLC
187 E Warm Springs Rd,
Suite B285, Las Vegas, NV 89119, USA

Website: https://workbookpress.com/
Hotline: 1-888-818-4856
Email: admin@workbookpress.com

Ordering Information:
Quantity sales. Special discounts are available on quantity purchases by corporations, associations, and others.
For details, contact the publisher at the address above.

ISBN-13:   978-1-956017-27-4 (Paperback Version)
           978-1-956017-28-1 (Digital Version)

REV. DATE: 04/08/2021

YOUR TRANSPORTATION TO YOUR DESTINATION

YOUR LIFE Journey

Is your life different and full of surprises that make you question yourself where you might have done wrong to deserve this? Let me take the time to congregate with you, for God have a great plan in mind for you. Just trust him, and you will end with a beautiful destiny.

*This book is dedicated to my children
Joel Hanson, Christopher Hanson, and Rudisha Hanson-Malcolm.*

MISS MARCIA P MATTIS

   I am always a happy person to minister to others in their time of need. The kingdom is my first priority; therefore, I possess the fruits of the kingdom, righteousness peace, Joy in the Holy Spirit,

THE AUTHOR
MISS MARCIA P MATTIS
BIOGRAPHICAL DATA

I was born on the Island of Jamaica; I am six of my mother's seven children. Most of my child wood schoolings were done in the country of my birth. In the year 1980, I had migrated to the Bahamas, an island where I live for several years; during the stay, I was blessed with three beautiful children of my own during these years, I develop my skills and talents in the years 1999 I move to the United Kingdom where I now resided and working as a senior support worker and a writer, my hobbies include music, singing and writing songs and writing different kinds of books and am also have a passion for Counseling,

INTRODUCTION

This book and its content are aimed to help the believer to endure their life journey and to be a reflection of the kingdom of heaven on earth while they are still living on earth, knowing there is always help from the kingdom of heaven at all time; you will be richly blessed as you read this book that the Lord has inspired me to write to all my reader. I hope it will inspire you to discover that your life journey has been designed for a purpose by God. We do not always have the choices we want. We only have to trust God always, and we will be blessed

Therefore it is always vital that we seek the kingdom of heaven daily, for this divine will to be done on earth as it is in heaven, for whatever we do. So let the kingdom of heaven be the main Centre of our heart. Whatever life throws at us, we must endure changes but never give up forget who you are in God, and as is offspring, we should keep our mind focus on our source with positives thinking; I pray that as you read this book that it will help you to walk in the perfect will of God, For GOD desire us to walk in his original plan, in this book I will be sharing a few bible characters and how they made their Journey. These characters are Joseph, who is a type of Jesus Joseph Journey will be explained in three P.s then Moses the delivers the last leg will be Jesus Mankind saviour,

Your transportation to your destiny

As children of the kingdom of heaven, we all have a different calling in life. Sometimes can be challenging experiences that cause us to wonder where God in all of this. Just know for sure he is with us; every step of the way, all we need to do is keep connected to him, make him our best friend, talk with him daily. He's always ready to speak with you even when you find yourself on the wrong side of life. When you are a temptation in life, run to your heavenly father, he is willing and waiting to comfort and forgive you and help put you back on the correct part. Our father has no grudge in his heart against us, neither looking to avenge us. He has a heart of compassion and forgiveness, and love for us. Most of all patient with our self and forgive our self also release your spirit of guilt and those lousy experience that you may have and do not allow the enemy to enslaved our soul to make you feel like nothing but failure, learn to celebrate our self and use critics to improve yourself, God believe in us that why he lives in us we are the very image of him and we are the temple of the living God, and it should be him only, anything else before him his an Idol I want to share some experience of a few characters from the bible and how they endure changes in their life, that led them to their destination the first person is Joseph sold as a slave by his brothers, in the final analysis, he executes the resource from the kingdom of heaven in the years of famine and the second Moses the great deliver of the Hebrew children to save the nation Go has chosen

We are children of God through Grace we are saved; as Children of destiny; we were born to do exploited and Dominate the earth realm by administrating the kingdom of heaven on earth; As God, offspring not the time know where God is leading us and why we are going in that direction, nevertheless, if we trust in God, know for sure that we are in the palm of his hand. Even though sometimes things may not seem understandable but fear not, for God is with us. Now I want to take you through a perfect example of this unknown Journey using Joseph's first characters whose qualities can be likened to a type of Jesus Christ. The last one is our messiah Jesus who finishes the race's final leg to restore mankind back to the father. In the book of Genesis, we will follow Joseph on his God-given Journey.

The unknown Journey

His father Jacob dwelt in the land of Cannon where his father Journey. Being seventeen years old, Joseph was a shepherd feeding the flocks with his brother, the sons of Balham. With the son of Zillah, his father wives, Joseph brought unto his father the ill report of his brother. Now Jacob loved Joseph more than any other of his children because he was the son of his old age so Jacob made him a coat of many coolers the others brothers been a shepherd they would stay in the field for days looking after their father flocks, one day Jacob called and said, Joseph go I pray thee see whether it is Well with thy Brothers and with the herd and bring me word again;

Therefore, Joseph went to the value of Hebron as Joseph came To Shechem something significant happens that brings me to an important point; this may be simple, but it's a turning point in Joseph life, the bible has it that a certain man who was wandering in the field saw Joseph, and he beholds him walking in the area the man said what seeks Throw Joseph said my brothers tell me where they are feeding the flocks he told him where they went. My points here is when God prearranges your destines and your life and gives you apart, you have to walk help will come along the way; I call this person who will assist you your destiny helper. For every crossroad in your life, there is always a destiny helper, and they come in unexpected form sometimes; we chase them away in ignorant for they do not look presentable in our sight,

look at these examples, Elijah, the prophet destiny helper, was a crow; we would call it an unclean bird, still God use it to feed his prophet; what if the man of God had resented the bird hungry would surely get the best of him, then we have the Shunammite woman she was out picking up firewood to cook her last supper for herself and son and then left to die for the land was experiencing famine, She could have quickly rebuked the man of God for it was her last, but she recognizes a destiny helper and then feed the man of God first and because of that God sustain her she had enough during the famine and after the famine,

Joseph Journey the three P, s.

I will explain each of these to you as I go along; because of Jacob's great love for Joseph, his brethren hated him bitterly, but Joseph had a dream and told his brother. So describing the dreams make them despise him the more, he said to them here I pray you this dream which I had for behold we were binding sheaves in a field and low my sheaf arose and also stood upright and behold your sheaves stood round about and made obeisance to my bunch his brothers said to him shall thou indeed reign over us? Then he dreams another dream that the sun and the moon and the eleven stars made obeisance to him, and he told his brothers. They hated him the more even his Father rebuked him and said shall I and thy mother and brother bow down before you? This makes his brother angry against Joseph, his father. The bible said he observes the saying,

The first P, Joseph cast in the pit

It's incredible how we feel excited and anxious to share our dream with the wrong people, not knowing we will create enemies, especially our close family. So my question is, was Joseph wrong to tell His brother his dream. Some may answer yes others may think differently. Still, I think this time it was the Right timing as it divinely and strategically opened a path to joseph destiny. It might surprise you how you can become a target even in your own family.

Let me take you back a bit Joseph started his journey when he went to see his brother and to bring food to his brothers. in the distance, they saw him coming here comes the dreamer was their words Let's kill him and say that some wild animal eats him then we will see what happen to his dream Ruben here the conspire among the other brother and try to protect Joseph.

It's no different in today's world; it's a problem when God promotes you over another. It can be a family member who is on the job a work college suddenly becomes the enemies they can try to jeopardize your life, even go to the extreme to get rid of you. Nevertheless, when God elevate you, there is no need to be afraid. The Bible said that the heart is deceitful above all things and desperately corrupt. Who can understand it?

No matter how one might conceal his wickedness sooner are later, it will manifest into reality. It was pure envy take hold of them to plot against their younger brother Joseph. Still, God had a plan in this; it was Joseph destiny. Hence, they strip and cast Joseph into the pit by his brothers. Before throwing him, they took his coat of many coolers, ripped it apart, and dipped it in animal blood to convince the father that He was killed by a wild animal; how long he was there in the pit was not mentioned then they sat down and ate bread. While they were there, they look a far of and saw a company of merchant coming; they decided to sell Joseph to these, Merchants on their way to Egypt; these men were another form of Gods divine destiny helper, there will be times Your Enemy Though they are doing, you harm they only help you to your destiny,

Joseph is symbolic to Jesus.

The symbolic action of Joseph and his brothers is the revelation of Jesus experience in similarity; Jacob's love for Joseph signified God's love. For his only begotten son Jesus, Joseph and Benjamin are of the same mother and father, Benjamin, the other ten brothers were Leo. Their handmaiden, the slave woman, the number ten, Represent the law, the Israelites are Jewish, and they are the most outstanding keeper on the law handed down to Moses. Jesus was a Jewish, so they were his brother daily they congregate in the temple lessoning to him speak about his father, and the words parse their heart, and they hate him the more and conspired to kill him, one of his Jewish brother who was his disciple sold him just like a slave Jesus was strip off his seamless robe, in other words, it was a specially made garment that was tailored specially for him, the lamb that they slay to dip the coat in representing Jesus, the lamb of God, I do believe when God place us in a family, it's connected to your individual ministry; if you can overcome your family, you are well on your way, for in your family, there is a Judas to Betray you of whatever they know about you And sell you out because they see you elevating, you might encounter the Thomas those who doubt your dream and vision and hope that it will not come to pass you also come across your peter who will deny you despite you trusting him very much, you can also meet, people who are always trying to avoid your company,

These characters can be purposeful in your life to transport you on your way to a glorious destiny. Jesus had them among his twelve disciples; it never stops him from fulfilling his purpose; they were all a part of his assignment to his destiny. Judas was the example of whether we can be trusted what motive he has toward Jesus; these are examples for us to take a note of the people we surround ourselves with; they either help us up or down, according to what you allowed to happen. Your Thames is where your strength or faith lies; doubt come to erase your faith dough is a powerful weapon to shake our faith, So I urge you all to be unshakable, for by faith we achieve from God, by faith in the word of God, we can defeat the enemy; the bible said if you have faith like a mustard seed, you can speak to the mountain to move. It will move, and Doubt comes to detour you from your true destiny. Peter is the testing of your character peter tested of his true love for Jesus, so will our love will be tested time after time in this present world everything that comes our way, we can overcome by the blood of the lamb and the word of our testimony we now have the full benefit of The transaction of the cross of Jesus, we had received our image back Jesus repurchased it when he took on flesh and condemn Sin in the flesh and nail it to the cross. *Therefore, we have to first recognize it to apply the correct principle to the test. Everything comes to remind us who we are and to ignite the power that lies within us; when you're tested, you will be announced, and in the end, you are still standing, having your loins guarded about with truth and fully dressed in the whole Armor you will be like,*

Jesus, when he was tested beyond all point, in the end, he was declared that indeed he's the son of God. This test comes unannounced that the reason the Bible said to be, Watchful be vigilant for the adversary. The devil comes like a roaring lion seeking whom he may devour; at the beginning of Joseph journey, Joseph never thought when he left home. He was bidding his father a long Goodbye. I should believe the brothers have a good discussion about him. Like the perfect plan come to past when they see these men coming, they took him from the pit, and Joseph was sold to the merchantmen; these men were Ishmaelite. They were, On their way to Egypt, the exact direction God had planned for Joseph To go, they were his Transport for his journey, even when life seems like you're in a pit keep hope alive God has not Forget about you; they may strip you of all your valuable things You may be hungry you may be naked, but you will become so hot to handle the pit won't be able to keep you, your Ishmaelite may seem late but keep hope alive use those time to know more about your legal rights as a kingdom citizen and the wait will worth it for they are still, coming for God hear your cry in the pit the same way he herds Joseph cry, So Joseph was taken out and sold for twenty pieces of silver and was taking to Egypt into fetter and chain as a slave; again, Joseph was sold to Potiphar, an officer of pharaohs, Captain of the guard. Now Joseph reaches the pharaoh's house, God in Joseph life every step of the way and the transportation to take him there. God needs to get him in the pharaoh's place to prepare for his family and the nation of Israel. Can you see how his Journey plan by God,

His life looks the same for you? You are a candidate for great Blessing; sometimes, we want every detail before making a move. But we need to trust our inner man, the voice of passive thinking, without being afraid of anything ever in the dark pit we are created to show God glory. We cannot tell whom we will meet and what state we will be in on this journey. Joseph was in stocks and chain still. He finishes nicely. Do not use the things of the world to measure up our life to prove whether we are blessed are not; what if they are taken away? Are we not still blessing? The only thing that Joseph had of value was his coat. It was taken away and ripped apart. Was he not still blessed with the presence of God? With God, we are the majority. He is our father, which means the source of all thing and provider in his word. He promises never to leave us nor forsake us; do we believe his word, Joseph reaches Egypt and a slave into Potiphar's house; the bible said *the Lord was with Joseph. He was a prosperous man, and he was in the House of his master the Egyptian soon Potiphar realized that the Lord was helping Joseph to be successful in whatever he did everything was going well with Joseph Potiphar liked Joseph and made him the overseer of his Household Joseph was put in charge of his house and all his property and fields. He was overseas over pharaoh wealth. Everything was to Joseph to decide; Joseph only wanted to please his master and his God. He was able to make choices of what he wanted to eat. God grace was with his always, when we walk in God's divined will and purpose; Joseph now been an overseer in his master house eat well,*

Sleep and wear the best of Egypt Clothing still that is not where Joseph journey end. Sometimes we get comfortable In Life thinking that we have achieved some great height. Have we ever stopped to think there might be more to life than where I am? We could ask the question, Is God finishes blessing me? We should never stop. The more comprehensive your vision becomes, and the more you are becoming yourself, God creates you to become; we should never stop until we leave this earth; we are little god the more we know who we are, the lesser we try to do things. Things will just happen naturally. The moment Joseph was made overseer in the house of his Master, The eyes of his Master Wife began lusting over Joseph for he was very elegant, and Hansom, his master wife, now have the opportunity of seeing him daily; her eyes become more desirable for Joseph she wanted Him to lie with her. Joseph refuses, for he values his relationship with God and is loyal to his master trust; this is how the enemy plans to distract us, especially the anointed ones. God will not leave us to the will of our enemy. His presence will always be with us. Jesus words to us his fair not when you enter into diver's temptation, With God; we are the majority for every trick he will make a way to escape. She was the next destiny helper to take Joseph to his next dimension; she never has her way with him; she was furious. You never know the person that will be used to push you to your next level; never underestimate anyone no matter who they are and what possession they hold in this life; they can be your next challenger. Joseph master wife speak lied on him he was cast in prison it was a divine trip to meet his next destiny helper two of the pharaoh servants,

the butler and the baker again the grace of God and the presence of the Lord was upon him for the Lord was with Him Joseph lifestyle was very graceful Joseph life pleases the guard of the person again he was made overseer in prison likewise God grace sustain him and bring him before men Joseph life is an example of one walking in true divine destiny, As blood wash children of God calls to the dominant, I *want to say it's not a comfort zone we enter into. We must not expect to babysit; we are children of the kingdom; we need to leave the religious church order and enter the kingdom domain; people are busy with church Duties— still, no genuine commitment to the kingdom of heaven. There is a wake-up call to dry your tears, possession yourself for a takeover if a man in chain and fetters can become overseas and governor you need to understand, what is the kingdom? A system of law and thinking makes the transition of spirit to flesh possible that allowed God to express himself in us. The domain operates on the vision and is birth by memory; we are the three-part man. We are a spirit with a soul living in an earthly body. The Holy Spirit and imagination implies the ability to form things that are not perceived through the five senses, and distorted mean twisted out of shape by guilt. The King and his kingdom and the children his governing and ruler ship of it knowing your true self his to now God for what in him his in us our thinking should line up with God original plan, so his kingdom will come on earth as in heaven,*

Second Ps Joseph in Prison

Here his Joseph cast in prison For bean loyal to God here is a young man who was a chain in fetters as a slave taken to Egypt to save a nation it was not known to Joseph what was the reason of his journey all of this focus was on how I can do this thing and sin against my God Joseph were put in prison because his faith was tried and his love for the God that his father thought him about he reaches the second (p) the prison. I love him because he stays connected to destiny by sticking to the kingdom of heaven by humility and loyalty to those in the leadership of his life; God's original idea was only in this is a symbolic dream that was never interpreted to this young man. Can we all say we know all about our destiny? Neither was Joseph; this takes me back to when men fell from grace in the Garden of Eden when Adam and eve committed S-Simple I-Instruction N-not taken? SIN, Father God has to come up with a plan to redeem man back to their first estate, God's original plan for mankind. After the plunge into hotter Darkness, the man was disconnected from their source the kingdom of heaven will use an example of a mother caring for a child in the womb signified us in God from the beginning. A baby in the womb survives to a card called the umbilical cord. The baby receives all supplies to nourish and stay alive. The connection from mother to a child; represents God and Mankind, and man gone independent from God leave the kingdom of heaven is an example of an unborn child connected to the mother with an umbilical the child depends on the mother.

When the child leaves the womb that supplies of nourishment are cut off, the child no longer gets its life supplies in that manner, for he is now gone from the womb, this same principle works with the kingdom of heaven man dependency was cut off in the garden of Eden when Adam fall and men plunged into darkness, the man Adam went independent and went astray and lose their science of direction to return home to the kingdom of heaven. What are men without their true purpose on earth? It is only a perfect mess, have you any doubt? Just look at the world today; sin is in demand; that's why God has to send his only begotten son Jesus came as an umbilical cord, a threefold that cannot be broken. The incision was done on an old rugged cross, his blood was shed, and the connection was made to return to the father care. Therefore, whosoever will have the opportunity to come true the true and the light, which is Jesus Christ, there is no other way back to the father but true Jesus. Therefore, if you are willing to come back home in the kingdom of the father, the Holy Spirit is waiting to restore your sense of direction. The prodigal son did come to his senses and said I will arise and go back home to my father; for there is a fountain fills with blood flown from

Emmanuel vain sinner plunge beneath the flow, lose all their guilt and stain.

Joseph stays in a relationship with defining God, just as Jesus remain in communion with his father in heaven while he was on earth. As Joseph remains in God favour fellow him even when he was falsely accused and was in prison, he was made to oversee in all things when you are in God perfect well favour will always be on you Joseph made himself content and let not his faith waver; there is no record in the bible,

Where he ever question God for his present God was always with him where God present his there his peace, reign, Yes even during your pain you can find Peace this Peace man cannot give its come from above its call the Peace that passed Understanding it cannot be understood by the mind of national man and an excellent example to a fellow of God instruction. What is our prison in this life? Is it your job, your home, your marriage you can make the difference now Gods present is with you, and that brings favour like Joseph as he was assurance, so will he comfort you in your prison we must not abort our destiny let find complete confidence and fellow his divine plan for our life, the time will come when your jail cannot hold you any more it has to release you into your next Dimension for Your life is a journey, Joseph's experience and the time spent in jail have come to an end, for God is about to show forth his glory through

Joseph for the next dimension that Joseph has possession himself for the pharaoh chief butler and chief baker, Joseph, met them, both. They have a dream and need an interpretation. Joseph noticed that their countenance was pale. He asks them what was wrong. They say to Joseph, we had a dream. There is no interpreter of it; Joseph said unto them do not interpretation belongs to God tell me, I will tell you that understanding will allow me to interpret those dreams for God's spirit. Just as Joseph said that the dream would happen in three days, the chief butler was restored to duty, but the chief baker was hung in three days. Joseph asks the butler to remember him before the king, but he did not because God has the timing to remember Joseph before the pharaoh;

The third P, s Joseph in the palace

There is always a perfect time in god schedule when he will promote you to your rightful place in life; now, Joseph, time has come to move on to his next dimension. The king had a dream none of his astrologers and magician could help him with his dream this brought back in remembrance they now remember Joseph, a man whom the spirit of God dwells he was taken from the dungeon person and was clean up and shaved dressed in fine clouding before seeing the king; he told Joseph his dreams the Spirit of God allowed Joseph to interpret the king's two dreams. The thing pleased the king, for he has never seen such a man whom the spirit of God dwells in, Joseph was promoted and reinstated to the governor of Egypt. He was made ruler over all of the land of Egypt, and Joseph makes his way into the palace beside the king, and he was given the king significant ring. Now Joseph fulfils his true purpose in Egypt, just like the interpretation of the pharaoh dream. The seven years of plenty begin the storerooms were filled until they lose counting it was more than enough then come the seven years. It gets so bad that lives stock were dyeing craps drying up no food to eat over the land of cannon. Still, in Egypt, Joseph was in charge over all of the food, and that the only land with food Joseph family heard that food was in Egypt their father sends the older brothers to buy food because the famine was great in the land of cannon, every livestock was dying out, Stop here with me. I just want to say distance does not change destiny and purpose; when God gives you a dream is a vision. No matter how far your enemy thought they got read of you,

God will make them find you to see it comes to pass. The first time before, it was Joseph who travels to feed his brother because they were hungry now the table turns hungry cause they to travel from far to find Joseph for food, and Joseph Fulfill the scripture which courted if your enemy hungry feed then and if they thirst give them drink,

Now Joseph brother travel to Egypt to find food; not knowing whom they were going to see, they came before the governor of Egypt to buy food who happen to be their very own brother Joseph surprise to them they never knew Joseph but Joseph recognize them God transform him and hide him so they could not now him before the proper time Joseph needed to know about his father and his younger brother and the dream was about to fulfill before their very eyes, Joseph find a way to question them without them knowing that he was the same brother that they had sold by now Joseph began to now his purpose of being into Egypt and were willing to forgive his brothers so are we as children of God should operate in the kingdom law and principle with a heart of forgiveness for the kingdom always forgive those that trespass against each other ,even when you're so call enemy are family member coworker are any one for that matter stand in your face learn to forgive It's more important to keep the instruction of God in our lives than to keep iniquity in our heart the bible ask us this question what shall suppurated you from the love of God only you can answer this question for you self-sorry to say many allowed thing and peoples to remove Gods presence from around them

Let's leave vengeance in the hands of God; he told us in his word it belongs to him he will repay Because the battle is the Lord no matter how long it takes, God word will not return to him void it Will accomplish what it was sent to do; you just want to know that when the green light of God is upon your life and his shining in your life from heaven that your time to shine has come, broken-hearted as Joseph Was he is going to see his very own dream fulfil before his very eyes. And Joseph was the Governor over the land he was the one who sold grain to all the people his brother came and bowed down themself before him with their face to the earth, The bible said Joseph remembers the dream and turn himself away and weep the word of God is sure in whatever way he chooses to reveal it. Surely it will come to pass with Joseph. His dream comes to pass. His brother did bow down before him. Joseph kept them all under guard for three days before saying to them, since I respect God, I'll give you a chance to save your lives if you are honest men stay here in jail and the rest of you bring your youngest brother to me then I will know that you are speaking the truth. You won't be put to death; his brother agrees and said to one another, we have been punished because of Joseph. We saw the trouble he was in, but we refuse to help him when he asks us that's why these terrible things happening; Ruben spoke up did not I till you harm not the boy, but you would not listen now we have to pay the price for killing him they did not know that Joseph could understand them since he was speaking through an interpreter Joseph turns away from them and cries

But soon turn back and talk again, then he had Simeon tied up and take away. The others watched Joseph give orders for his brother grain sacks to be filled with grain and for their money to be put in their sack he all so provide a portion of food for their journey home. after this was done, they each loaded the grain on their donkey and left; they had to stop for the night to rest and feed the donkeys; one of the Brothers open his sock to get some grain for the donkey, and surprising to him in the sack of grain, he saw his money bag, Here is my money, he told his Brother right here in my pack; they trouble with fear as they stared at one another and asked what God had done to us? When they return to cannon, they told their father Jacob everything that has happened to them. The Governor of

Egypt was rude and treated us like spies, but we told him we were honest men, not spies; we came from a family of twelve brothers. The youngest is still with our father in cannon, and the other is dead, then the Governor of Egypt told us I will find out if you are honest. Leave one of your brothers here with me while you take the grain to your starving family but bring your youngest brother to me to ensure that you are honest men and not spies. After this, I will let your brother goes free When the brothers started emptying their stock of grain, they found their money bag in them; they were frightened, so was Jacob he said they have already taken my sons Joseph and Simeon from me and now you want to take away Benjamin ever thing his going against me Benjamin speak up father trust me I will bring him back. But Jacob said, I won't let my son Benjamin goes down to Egypt with the rest of you. His brother is already dead, and he is the only son left.

I am an old man, and if anything happens to him on the way, I'll die from sorrow, and all of you will be blame; the grain was finish, so Jacob send them back into Egypt to buy more grain Judah replied the governor strictly warned us that we would not be allowed to see him unless we brought our younger brother with us, If you let us take Benjamin along with us we will go and buy grain but we won't without him Jacob asked why did you have to tell the Governor you have another brother you cause me much trouble they answer he asks many questions about us and our family he wants to know if you were still alive and if we have anymore brother all we could do was answer his question how could we now he would tell us to bring along our brother   Judah said to his father let Benjamin go with us and we will leave at once so none of us will starve to death I promise to bring him back safely, And if not you can blame me as long as I live if you have not wasted all this time we could already have there and back twice Jacob said if Benjamin must go with you take the Governor a gift of the fine things of our country Such as perfume honey spices pistachio nuts and almonds also take twice the amount of money for the grain because there must be a mistake when the funds were put in back in your socks take Benjamin with you and leave at once, when you go to see the Governor I pray that God all powerful will be good to you and that the Governor will let your other brother and Benjamin come back home with you the brother took the gift twice the amount of money and Benjamin they were worry because of the funds that were in their sack that the Governor would prison them and make them slave and take their donkeys, when they arrived

They make it be known to the servant in charge that they were here before to buy grain. Still, when we stopped for the night, each one of us finds in our grain sack the exact amount of money we paid. We brought the money back.

We don't know how put it in our sockets; his servant said, it's all right the God you and your father worship must have put the money there. Because I have received your full payment, then they brought Simeon out to them. The servant took them into Joseph house and gave them water to wash their feet; he also Tenders their donkeys; the brothers get their gift ready for Joseph at noon since they were going to eat there when Joseph came home, they gave him the gift they brought. They bowed down to him after Joseph had asked them how they were; he said, what about your elderly father? Is he still alive? They answer your servant our father is still alive and well, and they bowed again to Joseph. When Joseph looked around and saw his brother Benjamin said, this must be your younger brother, the one you told me about. God bless you, my son; then, Because of his love for Benjamin, he rushes into his chamber and weeps, then washes his face and return he was able to control himself and said serve the meal Joseph had prepared food and eats with his brother because he has forgiven them. Later, Joseph told them to fill their sack with grain as much as it could hold and put their money in the socks also put the silver cup in the stocking of the younger brother socks; the servant did as he was told early the morning the men were sent on their way with their donkey, but they did not reach far from the city when Joseph said the servant went after those men when you caught up with them

Say my master had been good to you, so why have you stolen his silver cup? When the servants caught up with them, the severance told the brothers precisely what Joseph had told them to say, but they said, sir, why do you say such a thing? We would not do anything like that; we even return the money we found in our grain socks when we return to Canaan, so why would we want to steal any silver cup or gold from your master house? Good, the man replied I'll do what you have said, but only the one who had the cup will become my slave; the rest of you can go free they open their sack the servant start Searching the sock, beginning with the older one first in the stocking of Benjamin. He found the cup they were all upset that they began tearing their clothes in sorrow they loaded their donkey and return to Joseph again they all bowed down to Joseph he said what have you done didn't you now that I would find out sir what can we do said Judah how can we say we are Innocent when God had shown we are guilty now all of us are slave Joseph said only the one found with the cup will be my slave the rest are free so Judah pleads for Benjamin, Judah went over to Joseph am said Sir you have as much power as the King himself and am only your slave please don't get angry if I speak, you asked us if our father was still alive and if we had more brothers so we told you our father is a very old man in fact he was already old when Benjamin was born, Benjamin brother his dead now Benjamin is the only one of the two brother who is still alive and our father love him very much, you order us to bring him here so you could see him for yourself we told you our father would die if we Leave him but you warned us that we could never see you Again unless our younger brother came with us, So we return and tell our father everything; now our father sends us back again, and with Benjamin Sir, our father reminds us that his favourites wife had given him two sons, One of them was already missing and had not been seen. So for a long time, my father thinks the boy was torn by some wild Animal said I am an old man if you take Benjamin from me and Per venture something happen to him I will die of a broken heart, that's why Benjamin must return with us to our father we do not want him to die of a broken heart, so please let me stay in his place

Joseph reveals himself to his brother

Since Joseph could no longer control his feeling in front of his servant, he sends them out of the room and Joseph reveal himself he cried so loud that the Egyptian heard him and told about it in the king palace Joseph asked his brother if his father were still alive. Still, they were too frightened to answer, and Joseph said unto them come near me. So his brothers go near him, I am Joseph you brother whom you sold into Egypt now, Therefore, be not grieved nor angry with yourself that ye sold me hither for God did send me to prepare life Joseph said to them for these two years hath the famine been in the land and yet there are five years in which there shall neither be earing nor harvest. And God sends me before you to preserve your prosperity on earth and save lives by a great deliverance. So now it was not you that sent me hither but God he hath made me a father to pharaoh and Lord of his entire house and a ruler throughout all the land of Egypt. *Joseph told them to go up to my father and said unto him thus said thy son Joseph for God has made me lord of all Egypt come down to me tarry not, and thou shall dwell in the land of Goshen. Thou shall be near me bring the children and grandchildren and your sheep, goat and all the cattle and everything else you own. I will take care of you during the next five years of famine; when Israel receives the message that*

Joseph was alive and the wagon he sends to take them back to Egypt, Israel spirit revive. Jacob Reaching Egypt,

Joseph brought Jacob (Israel) and presented him before Pharaoh then Jacob blessed Pharaoh, then the Pharaoh asks Jacob, how old are you? Jacob said the years of my pilgrimage are a hundred and thirty years

Hence, Joseph settled his father and brothers and gave them a possession in Egypt in the best of the land of Ramses (Goshen). So the number of the soul that came with Israel was sixty-six, for Joseph was already in Egypt. And his two sons and they were settled in Goshen as Pharaoh commanded for Joseph presented then to the pharaoh as shepherd now the children of Israel grow in numbers and Multiplying Jacob grew old when Israel saw Joseph sons, he asks who these sons are these Joseph said these are my sons whom God has blessed me with. Jacob blesses them all that day. Israel said to Joseph, behold, I am about to die. Still, God will be with you and bring you back to Cannon, the land of your father. Israel gathered all together and told them what will happen to them. Their descendants in the days to come to Joseph fell upon his father's face and wept over him and kissed so Israel die and after forty days of mourning for this is the numbers of regular days required for embalming the Egyptian wept and grieved for him as they would for royalty, So Joseph took his father back to the land of cannon to berried his father because he swears to his father to bring his body back to their fathers land and Joseph Live in the land of Egypt; he and his father household And Joseph lives a hundred and ten years and saw his third generation of Ephraim children and Marcher, the son of Manasseh, were born and raised at Joseph's knees Joseph said to his brothers

I am about to die. Still, God will surely take care of you and bring you up out of this land to the land he promised to Abraham to Isaac and Jacob, so Joseph died being a hundred and ten years old. They embalmed him, and he was put in a coffin in Egypt. Now a new king arose over Egypt who did not know Joseph or the history of his accomplishment. He notices that the people of Israel were many and very mighty and multiplying in number. So he makes it be known to his people that he has a concern and that they may rise against Egypt and join with Egypt enemies and defeat them, so the pharaoh put taskmaster over them to afflict the Israelites into bondage and great slavery their task was very hard to bear wherefore the children of Israel began to cry out to God for deliverance, The more pharaoh slave master afflicts the children of Israel, the More they grew in strength; the mighty army of God was increasing this makes the Egyptian more afraid, but God had a purpose in these people God was thinking of Nation for the Promises Abraham

He will establish a nation through him, and all nations would be blessed. I perceive God did not want Israel to get comfortable staying in Egypt and would not want to leave; indeed, that was not God idea for Israel. Therefore, God had to allow them to be enslaved in hard labour so when the time has come for them to leave, they will run with all their might to Escape slavery, For God has promised that they would be a great nation to their four father Abraham and God is a covenant-keeping God, as the Hebrews people *multiplying in great numbers it was making the pharaoh think evil against Israel, therefore, Pharaoh called for the midwives and*

commanded the midwives one by the name of ship rah and the other push and instruct them whenever the time of the Hebrew woman's come to give birth once it is a baby boy child you should kill him and preserve the girls, but God put fear on them they could not do it more over the Hebrew woman was very swift in delivering their babies God mission require quick action some times,

Especially when the enemy is standing at the door of your tent to devour the male child from creation again, the king get frustrated and ask the midwives to report to him the reason that the Israelites is still multiplying the Hebrew women are not like the Egyptian woman they are lively and swift in labour was their reply, so God dealt well with them he rewarded them the king change his plot and send out a decree to throw every male child in the river Nile. But during the order of killing these children, God find himself a family that would follow his leading for the saving of a male child that he would use years later to deliver his people, Israel, from the enslavement in Egypt,

Moses God Deliver

Here is another man with a great destination Moses, sometimes it seems when God have an excellent plan for you, the enemy moves closer to you; they become your neighbour Moses was born when the Egyptian became fearful of the Hebrews, for they were growing in great numbers and peradventure they would join with the enemy against Egypt. The present pharaoh has no history of Joseph and his faithfulness and works in Egypt. Still, God has himself a deliver from the house of the Levi, There went a man of the house of Levi and took to wife, a daughter of Levi. The woman conceived and dear a son when she saw him that he was a goodly child she hid him three months because the decree was sent out to kill the entire male child from the age of two years now this child had a destined with purpose like Joseph. The mother has instructed in her heart of love a plan that God has given her because God has seen her heart she purposes that her child will not be killed by this wicked decree that was sent out at her child-life she's not thinking death; she's thinking life, God gives her a plan to make a basket and how to dress it so that the crocodile would not be attracted to him, for in this basket his a messenger and in him was the message from God to Pharaoh, to let my people go, Israel, this person the chosen nation, as is mother skillfully make this ark of safety for the *prophet and place it in the river*

Nile the sister of, stood afar off watching and waiting to see what would be Done to him, and the daughter of Pharaoh came down to wash at the river. Her maiden walked along by the riverside, and when pharaoh daughter saw the ark among the flag, she sends her maid to fetch it. The moment the basket was open, the child cries out. It touches the heart of Pharaoh Daughter. This was the chance to be protected by the very enemy that seeks his life. She names Him Moses because he was drawn from the water; Who can fathom the ways of Gods; it was the last place pharaoh would be looking for his contender, especially with a message that no man in his right mind would say to a pharaoh, about his slaves without been kill instantly Moses eat the most delight full food and wear the best garment of Egypt for years, Let us not predict our destiny; we must depend on the movement of the move of God; when we try to figure out the next move, we will be frustrated just let the timing of God have his perfect way, and his will be done just as In creation when the spirit moves upon the face of the earth. God said, let there be when the spirit has complete control. We then think like God. We then see the act of God come to pass in our lives

The present pharaoh enslaves them for over four hundred and thirty years. They cried day and night to the Lord for help, but God was waiting for the right time to deliver them in the Meantime, growing mightily and strong. Moses was Nurse by his Mother for a while; she taught him about the true and living God, the God of their fathers. Moses was introduced by the pharaoh Daughter about their gods

This makes me know that his mother had committed him to God and told him about the God of their forefathers. I Admonish every mother make sure your children here about the true and Living God so when they go among unbeliever of their faith they will not be Persuade away from the truth; also parent give your children to God like Moses they are sounded by people every day who has no fear of God we may have to live with people who have different beliefs from us, so we have to be strong. Now that you are in the care of God, your Father, and he has a plan for your life, we all have a Journey to fulfill, and he can use whosoever he will; what if Moses mother did not let him go and live with Pharaoh daughter? Would he be out of the plan of God? It's Important to think with the mind of God; we will know God idea even if we have to let go of a loved one. I know Moses's mother loves him and desires her child to be home; instead, she gives him up to live rather than die. She had done her Godly duties while she had him. Parent, who are you training up? Is it a preacher or a prophet who are a great leader? Is it another Moses? Mother allowed your children when they make a mistake still love them be there for them the same way you do at any other given time

   I was told the story of the man who created the light bulbs. He was asked this question why is it that you make four thousand mistakes before you get it right. His reply was it was not four thousand mistakes. It was four thousand ways it will not work. An error can become a teacher; Moses living in the pharaoh world was not easy. The time comes for Moses to move on to the next dimension. Moses was about frothy years old one day,

   He went out to see his brothers and saw an Egyptian beating one of his brothers. Moses struck him and killed him; this news reached the ears of the pharaoh, so Moses has to flee. Moses went to the median and meets the daughter of the Priest of Median she was given to him for a wife they had two sons Moses was now a shepherd keeping his father law sheep's in the back desert the time has come for the children of Israel to be delivered from their enslavement therefor the Lord God about too appeared to Moses in a Burning bush of fire. God has heard the cry of his people and sending a delivery who will go to Pharaoh and give him a message and to deliver his people I believe God allowed Moses to run away and train him up to become a great leader God had to school him In the backside of the desert feeding sheep's sheep has no science of danger they always in trouble so was the Hebrew children they were sheep without a shepherd. In the bible, sheep Represent people. It was no better way to train Moses, but by using sheep, Israel was under hard labour just live, many people who are now in great ministry did not come up overnight; they had challenges along the way set back and disappointment

You sit with them and have a very long talk with them; maybe your tears would become empty from crying due to some of the embarrassing things they went true even in silence, but God brings them true. Never see yourself above another child of God you too can fall never talk down on the man are a woman of God when they do things differently from the way you thought it should be done get to know them and encourage them and

Become a true brother are a sister to them even when you may have a difference in perspective in what you believe we can all learn something from other because it's only one true Gospel, and that's the one Gospel that Jesus taught on Earth when he was here which is the good news of the kingdom of heaven we are many it is like a giant puzzle with thousands of pieces to complete it. Each of us has a piece some may have more than one pieces accordantly to one's talents and ability the bible give us a story about the people with different amount of skill *it's all for the glory of God so let's pay attention to what we have and let the next person work Independently, there is a suitable time for sharing your taught and revelation. Let us talk about Moses visitation; Moses is about to get a visitation from God for the time has come for Gods people to be delivered. The Lord God appeared to Moses in a burning bush and call him by name Moses, Moses. He said, here am I, and God said, take off your shoes from your feet, for where you are standing is holy ground. Then God introduces himself to Moses, I am the God of thy father the God of Abraham, the God of Jacob, so Moses hide his face for God for he was afraid to look upon God; this was a new experience for Moses, we too can experience this moment as long as we are called of God it may not be a burning bush. Whatever way God choose to talk to us and if we are not in communication with him it becomes hard to understand, And even become afraid like Moses; God is such a merciful God will make himself known to us God is not here to make us afraid of him but to allow us to make the right choice and take our rightful place on the earth territory, we all have on assignment on earth,*

Moses, too, was on a Journey from birth. God chose him from his mother womb to be the man he will use to deliver his people Israel. Moses life was already selected by God Moses never now but is about to find out his purpose the moment he says, here am I Lord, Moses takes the first step into his journey now God begins to make it clear to Moses. God said I have indeed seen the affliction of my people, which are in Egypt. Their cry has come before me because of their taskmaster for I know their sorrows and am come down to deliver them out of the hand of The Egyptians and bring them up out of that land unto a good land and large unto a land flowing with milk and honey's and after God finish talking to Moses how much God was concerned about his children been in sorrow day by day. They cry out to him daily for help, come now. Therefore, I will send thee unto Pharaoh that thou mays bring forth my people the children of Israel out of Egypt. If you notice in Joseph day, it never mentions once where God give him any instruction. Still, his presence was with him; it was God in a different form. God was the unseen master in his life now Moses had his instruction to go to the king of Egypt and say unto him the Lord God of the Hebrews hath met with us and now let us go into the wilderness three days journey to sacrifice to the Lord our God, In this action of delivering God people he had to face with the enemies he had to let pharaoh now who is the true God for years. He had a wicked taskmaster over them, but a covenant was made with Abraham and Isaac; Jacob God is a covenant-keeping God. He makes it clear to Moses God say I am sure that the king of Egypt will not let you go,

No, not by a mighty outstretch hand. There

is time you wonder why you pray and pray, and things remain the same. Don't give up; maybe God is about to take your enemy to the Red sea, but he needs something are someone that they will follow; when God is putting an end to something, he takes it from the root and destroys it all, and the quest goes on pharaoh was worn nine consecutive times by Gods messengers Moses and Aaron to let my people go so that they may go and serve me. The true and living God And God still saying today to many pastors and leaders let my people go let them worship me do not put my People in your small boxes, the Lord reveal to me that many of these churches are like an Aquarian or a fishbowl Pastor establish their own fishes tank and lock in Godchildren when God have an ocean for them to discover more profound things in him, we were called to do exploit(explosion)there can be no confinement between the wall of a building are religion all of the limitations this put mankind in custody they will not fulfil their God-given destiny no pastor no leader know your destiny we all now in parts for the secret about you is with God YOUR LIFE IS HID IN CHRIST IN GOD before the foundation of the world. Again Joseph and Moses went from one stage to the other, not knowing how the additional step would be when the almighty God is before you never fair the assignment now God allowed Moses to face pharaoh to deliver the message it was not easy for Moses the king that wanted to kill him for killing an Egyptian he has to now face him, Moses need God divine Intervention he told God that I have a speech impalements God gave him his brother Aaron to go with him how many time we try to bargain with God

But still is a merciful God the same love that God have for the Israelite it's the same for Moses he's not a partial God, the message was a message without apology God said let my people go so they can worship me the Almighty God, Today I decried and declared over your life, whatever or whoever acting as a pharaoh in your life that is stopping you are trying to stop you from pursuing your assignment on this earth for the kingdom of heaven to back up and back off and allow you to fulfill your God-given mission. He's the same God in Moses days, and he's the same today. God will do the same for you. Pharaoh heart was hardened because God did it, and he refused to let them go. God have a plan for the advisory in your life; do not be hasty when God make your enemies stay around you, for there is always a reasonable idea, for they that weight upon the Lord shall renew their strength you will mount up like eagle looking down on your accuser the higher you go in the spirit realms the enemies will have a challenging task to get you, for in the kingdom of heaven no weapon that forms against you shall prosper your God is a consuming fire After the nine plagues, the *pharaoh heart never changes the last acts of God in Egypt reaches the pharaoh heart when the angel of death passes over the nation of Egypt all the firstborn of Everything the Egyptian own from made servant to the firstborn of the animate even the nest hair to his throne of Pharaoh was smitten by the angel of death this bring Egypt into mourning and sorrow for a long time. The Table overturns a time when the Hebrew woman's Weep and mourn over their children as they watched them be taken off the Brest and cast into the river Nile;*

It seems as if God was not there. Still, the all seen eyes were overlooking, and his Ears heard their cry. God has a set time to end everything that is the reason he preserves Moses in the same river Nile for Moses represents all the other babes who died in the river for he will return and speak for them the same water that drowns those Hebrew children Moses flout on it straight into the Enemies camp the basket represent Gods ark of safety no Matter what storm in your life Protection available for you if you need it Gods is the ark of safety and pharaoh finally Release them to go and take their life stock their children and wives everything they have and go and worship your God he said and bless me before you go Moses. Still, God was not in any Negotiation with pharaoh Request time was expired and the Children of God time has come to be delivered is about to begin Pharaoh raised in the night he and his entire servant and all the Egyptians and all there was a great cry in Egypt for there was not a house where there was not one dead. And the king called for Moses and Aaron by night, and he urged them and sent them to go and worship their God; all the women's were instructed to borrow from all the Egyptian women gold and silver; they spoiled the Egyptians that night because they were afraid of the Israelites God. So Moses and the children of Israel started their journey from Ramses to Succoth about six hundred thousand on foot that was men besides children and six multitudes went up with them and flocks and herd and very much cattle. It may look hard when they started, but in the end, God has the last say he will not allow your enemies to triumph over you when he is in control some; time things hit you with all that it has,

And you still stay standing, maybe with a limp. Do you ever think why you did not get swallowed up by the enemy? Because God was carrying you in the palm of his hands, there were no tracks of your footprint in the sand for the enemies to Fellow. He never says that the journey would be easy. God Promises you when the journey comes to an ending, it will be a Victorious ending. You will have time with the Lord to Observe and remember and pass it on to your generation, for the Lord is a God delivered with a mighty strong hand. The Lord spoke unto Moses saying speak unto the children of Israel that they turn and encamp before PI- Zephon between Migdol and the sea over against Baa- Before it shall ye encamp by the sea For pharaoh will say the children of Israel they are Entangled in the land the wilderness hath shut them in. I will harden pharaoh heart that he shall follow after them and defeat the king and his army; this will bring honor upon me, and that pharaoh and all the Egyptian may know that I AM THE LORD. The Israelite did just as they were told when the king of Egypt was told that the Israelites had left him, and the officers change their mind about them. They said what we have done to let Israel go; we have lost our slave, so the king prepared his chariot and took his war army. They couldn't believe that the Israelite has gone from serving them; they were distraught, saying, why we have done this that we have let Israel go from serving us in this age. Today we do have consistent people in our life who thought they own us and not God; just learn from this you are just the target to lead them to their destruction where you will see them no more.

And pharaoh made ready his chariot and took his people with him. He took six hundred chosen chariots and all the chariot of Egypt and captions over all of them, and they went after them and overtook them camping at the seats is what I observe in my spirit that had to happen. It was like watching a suspense movie, wondering what next. I love the way God work; there will come a time when we will stop Running and wait for our enemies; God purposely stops them and make them camp out by the sea, for he's about to stretch out his intense harms as the Egyptian drew near the children of Israel become afraid .they had no idea what was about to happen. Hence, they cry out to God they begin to blame Moses in all ways they could. However, Moses said, fear not and stand still and see the salvation of the Lord it was a word in season for indeed our eyes shall behold and see the reward of the wicked even when they are coming with speed on wheel riding on horse God will take the chariots wheels off and lame their horses And when pharaoh drew nigh the children of Israel lift their eyes and behold the Egyptian marched after them. They were sore afraid, and the children of Israel cry out to God, Moses assures the people not to be frightened, for the Lord has said unto Moses I will fight for you, and he shall hold thy peace and the Lord said unto Moses, wherefore cries thou unto me? So speak unto the children of Israel that they go forward. Now Moses was commanded by God to lift thy rod and stretch out thin hand over the sea and divide it, and the children of Israel shall go over on dry ground through the midst of the sea. And behold, I will harden the heart of the Egyptian, and they shall follow thee.

I will get me my honor upon Pharaoh and upon the entire host upon the chariots and his Horseman and the Egyptian shall now that I am the Lord when I have gotten, My honor upon Pharaoh upon his Chariots and his horseman, The Angel of God which went before the camp of Israel removes and went behind them and came between the center of the Egyptian and Israel and it was a cloud of fire for the Israelite and dark cloud to the Egyptian but gave not light by night to them so that they came not near them all the night. The Angel represented God when the angel was at the front. It was God leading the enemy to their doom as well as taking his children to the Promised Land; now that They were next door to the promised land, God moves possession because he's about to roll up his sleeve he's about to fight I can hear God saying Vengeance his mine I AM, is about to repay so Moses did as God has commanded him; the water was divided on each side as a wall the children walk over on dry land. Still, Pharaoh Purpose to peruse them; they went after them all the host of the Egyptian they thought it was Peace and Safety but came sudden destruction. Your enemy doesn't leave you because you wish it to, but they will be eliminated when God said so there are times he will give you rest from them until he gets his honor upon them you will see them no more. Then God spoke to Moses again to stretch forth the rod again; if you notice Moses has nothing to say, he only complied with God's Instruction, God word declare, yea. However, I walk through the valley of the shadow of death

I will fear no evil thou art with me thy rod and thy staff they comfort me, Here was the rod in action it works in favor for the children of Israel and work against the Egyptian.

When the prophet Moses stretched forth the rod, he represented God's mighty outstretched hand because he said I will deliver you out of the Egyptian land with a mighty outstretched hand; Moses stretch forth the rod, and the children went over safe on the dry land. God told Moses to extend the rod again. The water begins to close on both sides; what a position to be in the middle of an Ocean bed closing on you that's the possession pharaoh. His host was in they all swallowed up at the bottom of the ocean and Godchildren go free, Believe it is not when their Tomorrow come they see them no more whatever God promise he indeed is gone a believer. Israel saw that great wonder that God did upon the Egyptian. They feared the Lord and believed his servant Moses after the great Deliverance they begin to sing songs of thanksgiving and praise unto God, *I will sing unto the Lord for the Lord hath triumphed gloriously. The rider hath thrown into the red sea the Lord his strength and song and became my salvation he is my God. He will prepare him an Inhabitation my God and I will exalt him the Lord is a man of war the Lord is his name thy right-hand O Lord become glorious in power thy right hand O Lord hath dash in pieces the Enemy who is like thee O Lord among* the Gods? Holiness is fearful in praise doing wonders. As the people of God, there is a time when we seem to forget the things that God has done for us; we all allowed things to make us suddenly lose focus of the blessing on the things God has done for us and the shame he covers and save us from then people goes back to our old lifestyle. After all, God has done for Israel just for a drink of water,

They begin to grumble and complain and greave the heart of Moses and God after Moses brought them across the red sea into the wilderness; it was just three days then they came by Mariah. The water was better to drink and, Moses cried unto the Lord, and the Lord showed him a tree and told him to chop it down and throw it into the water, and it became sweet. How easy for them to forget that entire great Wonders at the red sea in three days and because of their Behavior what would take those seven days take them frothy years. Hence, God has to prepare us for our blessing; if we get it before we are ready for it, we will only make a mess. The Egyptian attitude and way of thinking determine the outcome of their life for the Israelites; all of the rebellious spirits of Egypt would have gone into the Promised Land with them; the only thing they would need is a pharaoh. But, God love his people, the children of Israel; they had to retrain in the wilderness before entering the Promised Land they took their Journey from Elam.

Thus, the congregation of Israel came into the wilderness of sin, which is between Elam and Sinai on the fifteen days of the second month after their departing out of the land of Egypt. And the whole congregation murmured against Mosses, and Aaron said unto them would to God we had died by the hand of the Lord of Egypt when we sat by the fleshpot and when we did eat bread to the full for he has brought us forth into the wilderness to kill this whole assembly with hunger, Then said the Lord unto Moses behold I will rain bread from heaven for you. The people will gather a specific rate every day that I may prove to them whether they will walk in my law or not.

And it shall come to pass that on the six-day they shall prepare that which they bring in, and It shall be twice as much as they gather daily, And Moses and Aaron said unto the children of Israel at even then ye shall know that the Lord hath brought you out of the land of Egypt. And in the morning then He shall see the glory of the Lord for that he heard you're murmuring against the Lord and what are we that he Murmuring against us. And Moses said the Lord shall give in the evening flesh to eat and in the morning bread to the full for the Lord has heard your murmuring against him and what are we? Your murmuring is not against us, but the Lord God and Moses speak to the children of Israel come near before the Lord for he heard your murmuring and it comes to pass as Aaron speak unto the whole congregation of Israel that they look toward the wilderness and behold the glory of the Lord appeared in the cloud. The Lord said to Moses I have heard the murmuring of the Israelites; speak to them saying at twilight you shall eat meat and between the two evenings you shall be filled with bread: and you shall know that I am the Lord in the evening quail came up and covered the camp. In the morning, the dew lay round about the camp. And when the mist had gone behold upon the face of the wilderness, there lay a small round and flake-like thing, as fine as hoarfrost on the ground. When the Israelite saw it, they said one to another, Manna, for they did not know what it was. And Moses said to them this is the bread which the Lord has given you to eat, God has supplied all their need that they ask for and more, yet because of what they use to in Egypt and accustom to their spirit were corrupt they eat sleep and live in mourning and Complaining they couldn't see that they have a loving father who will not forsake them,

and has just taken them out of abuse in Egypt; the only thing they could do to thank God was to Grumble and complain against Moses and God, his anger was kindled, and God had to start killing out those Rebellious ones and save the future Generation it is a dangerous thing to fall in the hands of an angry God. But thank be to Jesus, who is our mediator between God and us; it is not enough to say I love God, but all so know that he first love you and is seated well with him in heavenly places in Christ Jesus that is where a believer start their new life in Christ please children of God let us learn from. Thus it is God who fights for his children and make provision for them. God kill out a whole army and a king to free Israel from bondage, later God had to kill out the older head of the Israelite to save another generation, all because of the spirits call rebellion, and unbeliever Israel makes it seems as if God cannot provide for his children their mind were still in Egypt and the things they used to get at their fingertip. The provision from heaven for Israel, the bread Manna, was like Coriander seed white and tasted like honey wafers. Forty years in the wilderness and they never knew hungry God provided every day fresh Manna except on Friday they collect twice the amount for two days the Sabbath and God keep it fresh even when they keep on provoking God with their behaviour, God spoke with Moses to come up to the mountain to talk with him and there God told Moses to get the people to wash themself to come before him at mount Sinai as soon as the presence of God came on the mountain the thunder and lighting the people were afraid and back away from God present telling Moses

you speak to God and then speak to us after God talk to Moses and the people said with one voice they all shout whatever God say we will all do

Israel went independent on God as if they could please God in their strength you may ask how did they independent on God after God call Moses on the top of Mount Sinai in a cloud and write the ten commandments, Then the Lord said unto Moses returning quickly for the people which thou brought out of the land of Egypt have corrupted them self they have turn aside quickly out or the way which I commanded them they have made themselves a molten calf and have worshipped it and have sacrificed their unto and said these be thy god, this was the spirit of independence ,showing up again, from Egypt unto mount Sinai they experiencing the Grace of God, this statement whatever the lord says we will do this is where Grace was put aside for they respond we can do it on our own until they begin to do their own thing and making a graven image for their God leaving the Grace of the almighty God,

God anger wax hot, and three thousand was ill at the foot of the mountain Moses plead to the lord did you bring them out to slay them in the hill, so Moses ask God to turn and change his Mind of the evil against his people and remember the Covenant that you make to our forefathers, Please, children of God, we need not fight our battle or serve strange God; we are now in the dispensation of Grace, a better promise and a better covenant we are now reinstated to our original state, the kingdom of heaven Jesus has redeemed us from the curse of the law

Joshua pick up the bottom

After the death of Moses the servant of the Lord it came to pass that the Lord speak unto Joshua the son of Nun, Moses m Minister saying, Moses, my servant is dead now, therefore, Arise go over this Jordon thou and all these people unto the land which I do give to them even to the children of Israel every place that the soul of your feet shall tread upon that have I given you as I said unto Moses from the wilderness and this Lebanon even unto the great river the Euphrates all the Land of the Hittites and unto the great sea towards the going down of the sun shall be your coast. There shall no man be able to stand before thee all the day of thy life; as I was with Moses so I will be with thee, I will not fail thee nor forsake thee. Be strong and of good courage, for upon this people shall thou divide for an inheritance the land I swore unto their father to give them. Only be thou strong and very courageous that thou Mayes observe to do according to all the law which Moses my servant commanded turn, not to the right hand or the left that thou Mayes prosper whithersoever thou go This book of the Law shall not depart out of thy mouth., thou shall meditate therein day and night that thou Mayes observe to do according to all that is written therein for then thou shall make thy way prosperous and then thou shall have success. Have I not commanded thee? Be strong and of good courage; be not afraid neither be thou dismayed for the Lord thy God is with thee.

The Lord gives Joshua the words of assurance God is constantly reminding his children of his promise and comfort them.

Moreover, he is a covenant-keeping God; he has promised their forefather the land to inherit. So Joshua commands the officers of the people to prepare for Victory for within three days ye shall pass over this Jordon to Go to possess the land which the Lord your God gives you to possess it. And Joshua, the son of Nun, sends out of shatter two men to spy secretly, Saying go view the land and they went into a harlot's house name Rehab and lodged there. Now some way, it reaches the king of Jericho's ears that these men were hidden in the house of a harlot and that they came by night to spy out the land, and they are the children of Israel. So the king of Jordon send to Rehab to bring forth the men that come to thee knowing that they come to search out all the country, but she did not give them up she hides them later that night Rehab went up to the roof where they were hiding, She said unto them I know that you're Lord, has given you the land and that terror is fallen upon all the inhabitants of the land faint and us because of you for we had heard how the Lord dried up the water of the red sea for you when ye came out of Egypt and what ye did unto the king of the Amorites that were on the other side of Jordon Siphon and Gog whom ye utterly destroyed, and as soon as they heard these things their hearts did melt neither did there remain any more courage in any man because of you for the Lord above and in the earth beneath, The Journey of the children of Israel was structure by God, and he chooses the way he would use for them to travel,

A harlot name rehab that hides his people never thinks you are wrong that God cannot use you for His purposes. Allowed the Holy Spirit to direct your life, your part to only be available during you're available; things can change for your good. Was there any other in the land whom God could have used to hide these men? Instead, because she shows kindness to them, she was able to ask the men to save her household never Judge anyone because you may know something about them. Sometimes they may be doing things not pleasing, but God is a merciful God even if it's you, the mercy of God endured forever. Again, the two men returned and descended from the mountain and passed over and came to Joshua, the son of none, and told him everything that occurred to them. They said indeed the Lord hath delivered all the land into our hands, for even all the country's Inhabitants do faint because of us. We cannot tell the things that God will do once he chooses you for a service he will kill to make his word comes to pass for who can battle with the Lord Israel journey show us we have to have a Makeup mind and that we will be opposed by many Adversaries and fear will take us but just. Remember he will never leave you nor forsake you; he who began a good work will complete it. Joshua said unto the people sanctify Yourself for tomorrow the Lord will do wonders among you and Joshua speak unto the priest, saying, take up the ark of The covenant and the Passover before the people. They took up the Ark of the Covenant and went before the people, and the Lord said unto Joshua this day will begin to magnify thee in the sight of all Israel that they may know that as I was with Moses, so I will be with thee

Thou shall command the priest that bears the Ark of the Covenant saying when ye have come to the bank of the water of Jordon ye shall stand still in Jordon. Again God is about to show his children his mighty outstretch hand of wander by selecting a priest to carry the ark of the covenant before the people to cross Jordon water. As the priest's feet step into the water, the water divided bank to the bank.

They cross over on dried land; therefore, they pick up twelve stone and a place to let the next generation know what the God of Israel had done for them before they inherited the Promised Land and how they were tested and tried while in the wilderness, there were sacrifices that were made. The children Of God face trial today in a different way, but if we allow God to fight our battle, God will fulfill his promise; he never leaves anything half finish, weeping may endure for a season, but our joy comes in the morning light recognition always comes after a great victory for everyone to see and hear, all great men and women in the bible become recognize when their battle was over. So when God makes the ears of those who here tingle. We all have people around us who never want us to inherit our promised land. Still, thru many danger toil and smear, we have already come for we are people of destiny and purpose we should believe the report of the Lord for the adversary always reach with sad information to cause us to take our focus off God But the word of God assures us that there is no temptation common among men that God has not already make way for us to escape; we always have promised to lean on.

    Jordon cannot stand in our way when God lead the way just as pharaoh and all his host end up at the bottom of the red sea, that same red sea that takes Israel over on dried land Israel was unstoppable as they move forward and be of good courage. God has designed Israel's destiny because he knew the way true the wilderness. Yes, they make foolish mistakes, and by doing the wrong thing, God anger kindled against them, but he could not completely destroy Israel, for he values his word for true this nation the tribe of Judah, the messiah will come to redeem all nation *the Greek and the Gentiles God also promises Moses when God send him to get his children out of Egypt because he wanted to make them a royal pries hood on the mind of God as kings and priest of the kingdom of heaven Israel today because of Israel we are now royal pries hood and a set-apart people we are here on earth to show forth the kingdom of heaven as his dear children, there is the moment we feel like Israel going around in a circle just like Israel in the wilderness, for forty years, the children of Israel walk-in The wilderness till all the people that were men of war which came out of Egypt were all died because they obeyed not the voice of the Lord swore that he would not show those older generations the land which the Lord declared unto their father that he would give us a land that flowed with milk and honey, disobedient his very dangerous it will keep you away from the privileges of the kingdom of heaven your promise inheritance in the kingdom of God it can close your doors to your most tremendous success and cause you more pain, Now Joshua circumcises the children of Israel again and they have their Passover*

And it came to pass when Joshua was by the Jordon that he lifted his eyes and look behold there stood a man over against him with his sword drawn in his hand and Joshua went unto him saying unto him Art thou for us or our adversaries and he said nay but as the captive of the host of the Lord am I now come and Joshua fell on his face to the earth and did worship and said what said thou Lord unto his servant and the captain of the Lord host said loose thy shoes from thy foot for the place where on thou stands is Holy and Joshua did so and they prepare the priests and the ark and the trumpet of rams horn before the ark of the Lord and he said unto the people pass on and compass the city The Lord came to lead Israel into victory to possess the promised land and as they all march around for six days then the seven days they rose early in the morning about the dawning of the day and compass the city after the same Manner seven-time only on that day they compass the city seven-time then Joshua commands the people to shout for the Lord hath given us the city the wall came falling as they were Command by Joshua. They utterly destroy Everything in the city, both man and women, young and old and ox and sheep and ass with the edge of the sword But for Rehab and her household, her father and mother, her brother and sister and the grandchildren all that had been saved. The city was burned with fire only the Silver and Gold and the vessels of brass. Of iron, they put into the treasure of the house of the Lord. Still, the children of Israel were command not to take any of the accursed things to keep you from the accursed so that the camp of Israel will not become a curse,

Now Joshua sent men to spy out the land; the report let not everyone go up but let about two or three hundred men go up to smite AI because they are few. But there were disobedient was among them an accurse things were among them in the Centre. How much do we know that we cause the curse to come upon us because of disobedience they went up usual not thinking that God was angry with them how many time we go against God word and expect him to give us what we want and when it doesn't happen we allowed hour flesh to run our life into doing things ungodly things here was Israel gone to fight AI God Watch them slay Israel.

They fled before the enemies when it was to be the other way around all because of one man who allowed his flesh to master him and greed take over so much time we take God for granted and forget that he is a holy God and his word his A and Amen what he said his what he means God will not become unholy just because we are his chosen ones what, An example would be showing us to the fellow we pay a lot of prices that could be avoided; yes, Jehovah is merciful, yes, Jesus is forgiven we learn the hard way because of choices we choose he could have saved them. Still, they would do the same thing again and expect him to give them victory again, as children of a holy God, let us desire to be obedience children, and we will eat the fruit of the land. Israel lost thirty-six men that day, and the heart of the people melted and become has Water O Lord what shall I say when Israel turned their back before their enemies. So Joshua rent his cloth and falls to the Earth upon his face to the ground before the ark of the Lord

Until the eventide, he and the elders of Israel put dust upon their heads. And Joshua cry to the Lord and the Lord said unto Joshua get thee up wherefore lays thou thus upon thy face?

Israel has sinned, and they had also transgressed my covenant which I commanded them for they have even taken of the accursed thing and have also stolen and dissembled. They had put it even among their stuff. Therefore, the children of Israel could not stand before their enemies but turn their back before their enemies because they were cursed neither will I be with you any more except ye destroy the accursed thing from among you then God said to Joshua get up and sanctify the people and yourself again tomorrow for thus said the Lord God of Israel there is an accursed thing among in the O Israel thou canst not stand before thy enemies until ye take away the accursed thing from among you. And it shall be that he that is taken with the accursed thing shall be burned with fire he and all that he hath because he hath transgressed the covenant of the Lord and because he hath wrought folly in Israel. Joshua Calls and gathers all family to their tribe. Joshua said unto Aachen, my son give I pray thee glory to the Lord God of Israel and confess unto Him and tell me now what thou hast done *hide not it not from me. He answered Joshua and said, indeed, I have sinned against the lord of Israel and thus and thus have I done Aachen own up to his sin action and told the man of God everything and that the accursed things were hidden in his tent. They took them out of the tent and brought them to Joshua and unto all the children of Israel and laid them before the Lord and Joshua gather all the children and life stock*

Silver and the garment, and Joshua said, why you have trouble the Lord and all Israel stoned them and burned them with fire. Let's use this as an example when even you think that you want to sin against God, think about your family and your Generation sin do not only affect you it comes with a price that affects those around you and can even cause death let us be mindful there are consequent to pay when we disobedient God Command to obey his better than to sacrifice let not our flesh Causes us to sin let us conduct yourself honestly and adequately as in the light of day not in carousing and drunkenness not in sexual promiscuity and irresponsibility not in quarrelling and Jealous but cloud yourself with the Lord Jesus Christ. And make no provision for the flesh concerning to improper desired. Let's take our assignment serious God is looking for serious people to take the gospel of the kingdom to the end of The earth; the journey of Israel is an example for us today now how you are and know your God and the love that he has for us there is nothing he would not do for us all we have to do is walk in our divine calling

Whatever we face, Jesus faces it with us; his promise is true he will not leave us nor forsake us; our body is Gods temple, protect it and make it remain holy unto him, which is our Reasonable service. The word of God admonishes us that there is now no condemnation to them which are in Christ Jesus who walk not after the flesh but after the spirit. We will not fulfil the lust of the flesh when mankind separated them from God; it caused Jesus to die, it cause Cain to kill Able. There are thousands of other examples of what sin affects, whether physical or spiritual death

Total Isolation from God to be carnal-minded is death, but being spiritually minded is life and peace. Therefore people of God, lay aside every weight that easterly set us and runs this life with patent looking unto Jesus, the author and finisher of our faith; there is a time coming when men kind will have to acknowledge that Jesus Christ is Lord why not do I know that you will escape the embarrassment of hearing too late for God Judgment has already set, and their life has been lost; yes, God is faithful, but mankind can resist the call of the spirit of God and his son death on the cross. Until it's too late

Israel sin and the Lord was displeased they transgressed the Commandment that god give *them, they were not able to live up to the ten commandments which is the law, thanks be to Jesus who ransom us from the curst of the law now we are on the other side of the cross, Let's not used our freedom as a license to commit sin, but to know the Grace of God help us to live and believe right knowing we have been love with an everlasting love of our father. He proves it to us by giving his only begotten son to save us from death, hell and the grave, Is any dough in your mind about the letter of the law that it kills? Take a look at the children of Israel. The bible said that God could not provide them with victory in the presence of the enemy, for there was sin in the camp, not until they were clean from their sin before they could get their victory. So they went from city to city and country to county and valley to valley and mountain to mountain and burned it with fire and killed the people that live there with the edge of the sword and take their Kings and hang them on trees from day till dawn and inherit the land as the Lord God was with them.*

And there was much to achieve for God has promised them all these land, but their obedience to God counts in all their victory; we should never think that God will smile at our Disobedient because of grace, but Jesus stand in our place and intercede on our behalf, reminding our father as he strength out is nail scar hand in the presence of God saying father remember I died for them, for Israel they did not have this privilege. Still, the Lord God kept his promise and gave them their rightful inheritance until this day; their Journey was victorious. The word said there was no feeble one among them. They kept fighting and multiplying in numbers; most of all, their leaders, Joshua, stayed with the Lord to give them the command that led them to a great victory in battle old age never stop Moses. It did not stop Joshua when he dies; he was one hundred and ten years old; the bible said to be not weary in well-doing. Joshua was faithful unto death, and so was Moses that was before him we as children of God our challenges may not be like Moses and Joshua but are we willing to stand for what we believe in, which is the true and living God and be not tangle in the yoke of fear and dough and intimidation the lies of the devil, but know that we are seated with Christ Jesus in heavenly places, above all principality and power from once we were before Jesus take us from

JESUS THE CHRIST AND IS JOURNEY TO OUR SALVATION

Jesus also was sent an assignment that takes him on a journey. He is the greatest of all Jesus the Christ. He's the only perfect example in the bible. Although his lifestyle causes the so-called religious people to fight him, Jesus came to earth as the very express mind of the father, God. His assignment is to return what Adam lost in the Garden. Adam lost the kingdom and all access and the key to the kingdom and the entire human race.

Everything Complete went into disorder, so Jesus mission was to restore his father's original plan for mankind back to its original state; image man was in trouble, the first thing that had to be done was to give him an earthly body actual the birth of an earthly body He needed an earthly body on the earth to make him legal to begin this assignment. So God provided a virgin girl named Mary. This Holy Spirit visits her and deposits the seed of God in her womb before she was espoused to Joseph, her husband; she was found with the child of the Holy Ghost. But while Joseph thought on these things behold the angel to the Lord appeared unto him in a dream saying Joseph thou son of David fear not to take unto thee Mary thy wife for that which is conceived in her is of the

Holy Ghost and she shall bring forth a son and thou shall call his name Jesus. For he shall save his people from their sin now, all this was done that it might be fulfilled which was spoken of the Lord by the prophet saying a virgin shall be with child and shall call his name Emmanuel which being interpreted God with us.

Then Joseph, her husband being a just man and unwilling to make her a public example, was minded to put her away privately. So the word conforms, his coming, for a child his born unto us a son is given and the government shall be upon his shoulder. His name shall be called Wonderful Counselor the Mighty God the everlasting father and the prince of peace of the increase of His Government and peace there shall be no end upon the throne of David and upon his kingdom to order it and to establish it with judgment and with justice from henceforth even forever the zeal of the Lord of the host will perform this for unto us is born this day in the city of David. This saviour is Christ the Lord. And it came to pass in those days that there went out a decree from Cesar Augusts that the entire world should be taxed. This Taxing was first made when Cyrene's was Governor of Syria. So all went to tax everyone into his city, and Joseph also went up from Galilee out of the city of Nazareth into Judaea unto the city of David which is called Bethlehem because he was of the house and lineage of David, to be taxed with Mary his espoused wife being great with child. So it was while they were there the day were accomplished that she should be delivered, and she brought forth her first son and wrapped him in swaddling clothes and laid him in a manger.

This is the announcement of the saviour into the world, Jesus Christ our King,

Now when Jesus was born in Bethlehem of Judaea in the day of Herod, the King behold there came wise men from the east to Jerusalem Saying where he that is King of the Jews is? We have seen his star in the east and come to worship him. So when Herod the King has heard these things, he was troubled and all Jerusalem with him. Herod inquired where Jesus was born, and when he gathered all the chief priests and scribes of the people together, he demanded of them where Christ should be born; the message was told to him that it was in Bethlehem of Judea for thus it is written by the prophet. Jesus sent them to Bethlehem and said, Go and search diligently for the young child. When he has found him bring me word again that I may go and worship him also When they have heard the King, they departed and lowed the star which they saw in the east went before them till it came and stood over where the young child was when they saw the star they rejoiced with exceeding great joy. And when they went into the house, they saw the young child with Mary, his mother and fell and worshipped him. When they had opened their Treasure, they present unto him gift Gold frankincense and Myrrh and God have worn these man in a dream not to return to Herod they departed into their own country God make a fool out of him. Herod has been a king does not make him Lord over the King of all kings then the angel of God appeared to Joseph in a dream to flee with the young child and his mother to Egypt there were there until the death of Heard

That it might fulfil out of Egypt, have I call my son. When Herod saw that he was mocked by wise men, he was furious and outraged. He sends soldiers to kill all male children in Bethlehem and in all that area who were two

John prepared the way

In those days came John, the Baptist preaching in the Wilderness of Judaea repent for the kingdom of God, is at Hand. Now John was Baptizing people in the Jordon river John told the Sadducees and Pharisee's ho generation of vipers to flee from the wrath to come I indeed baptize you with water unto repentance. Still, he that comes after me is mightier than I whose shoes I am not worthy to bear shall baptize you with the Holy Ghost and fire John was announcing Jesus arrival, then Jesus came from Galilee to John to baptize him. John refuses to Baptize Jesus; John said, It is I who need to be Baptize by you and you come to me, but Jesus said suffer it to be so now for thus it becomes us to fulfil all righteousness then John baptized, now Jesus, when he was baptized, Jesus went up Straightway out of the water and lowed the heaven were opened unto him and saw the spirit of God descending like a dove and light am him. And the voice from heaven saying this is my Beloved Son in whom I am well pleased then Jesus was led into the wilderness to be tempted of the devil after forty days and forty night of fastening were finished, and the devil knew that Jesus were very hungry the devil had no regard of the son of God Jesus finish crucifying his flesh and Putting it under control, this was nothing to the devil his purpose was too defeated Jesus, but Jesus was filled with the

Spirit and the word Jesus,

Combine the Spirit and the words after the devil told him to command the stone into bread but Jesus answers the him and said it his Written Man shall not live by bread alone but by every word that proceeded out of the mouth of God, Jesus again was tried he was taken up into the holy city and Set on a pinnacle of the temple and said unto him if thou be the Son of God cast thyself down for it his written he shall give his angels charge concerning thee in their hand they shall dear thee up lest thou dash thy foot against a stone Jesus said unto him its written thou shall not tempt the Lord thy God, for the third time he takes Jesus on an exceeding high mountain and Showed him all the kingdom of the world and the glory of Them and said all these things will I give you if thou will fall and worship me again Jesus rebuke him saying get thee hence Satan it his written thou shall worship the Lord thy God and he only shall thou serve, then the devil leave him and the angel came and ministered unto him. Yes, when we are an overcomer by the blood of Jesus Christ, we will be ministered to by angels, for we are the blood wash saints,

Jesus Mission Statement

From that time, Jesus began to preach and say repent for the kingdom of heaven is at hand; Jesus was making it known that the domain that Adam lost in the Garden has returned, then Jesus walks by the seaside of Galilee, where he began to choose his Disciple. Jesus saw two brothers, Peter and Andrew. He calls them to follow him and said I will make you a fisher of men. Then James and John were two brothers, and they were the sons of Zebedee; they were mending their fishing net with their father, and Jesus calls them and said fellow me. So Jesus went about Galilee preaching the gospel of the kingdom and healing all manner of sickness and all form of the disease among the people. His fame went throughout all Syria, and they brought unto him all sick people that were taken with diver's diseases and torments and possessed with the devil and those which were lunatic those that have palsy and healed them all. So they followed him. A great multitude of people from Galilee and from Decapolis and from Jerusalem and from Judie and from beyond Jordon Jesus taught the people on the Mountain the law of the kingdom of God and how they should live and forgive each other and continued to heal them from all manner of diseases that it might be fulfilled which were spoken by the prophet Isaiah Saying himself took out infirmity and bear our sickness now when Jesus saw a great multitude around him Jesus gave the command to depart unto the other side.

And of the certain scribe came and said unto him master I will fellow thee whatsoever thou goes, and Jesus said unto him the foxes have held. The bird of the air have nested, but the son of men hath not where to lay his head, And one of his disciples said unto him Lord suffer me first to go and bury my father, Jesus reply let the dead bury their dead Jesus enter a ship. His disciple fellow him, and there arose a great tempest in the sea. Jesus was having a rest and was sleeping, his disciples were afraid and waked Jesus and said Lord save us we perish Jesus reply why are ye fearful O ye of little faith, Jesus arose and rebuked the sea, and there was a Great calm The men marvel saying what manner of man his this that even the wind obey him after leaving the boat Jesus met two-man possessed with the devil from the tomb exceeding fierce so that no man might pass by that way and behold they cried out saying what we to do with thee Jesus thou son of God have? Art thou come hither to torment us before time? Now Jesus was a good way off, and there was a heard of many swine feeding their swine the spirits plead to Jesus to cast them into the herd of swine and behold the whole Herd of swine ran violently down a steep place into the sea and perish in the water, and the keeper of these swine fled and went their way into the city and *told ever thing and what was befallen to the possessed of the devils and behold the whole city came out to meet Jesus, and when they saw him they be sought him that he would depart out of their coast Jesus manifesting the works of the father,*

Not many people enjoy him being around, but Jesus did not let them stop him. He sets out to obey and carry out his father assignment; Jesus enter into a ship and Passover and into his city they Brought to him many that were sick, and they brought a man to Jesus he was sick of the palsy and lying on a bed and Jesus seeing their faith said unto the sick of the palsy; son be of good cheer thy sin be forgiven thee there were sure of the scribe said within themself this man blasphemed now Jesus knew there thought said think he evil in your heart? Is it not easier to say thy sin be forgiven thee or to say arise and walk but that the son of men hath power on earth to forgive sin. Jesus turned to the sick man and said, take up thy bed and go into the house and the man arose and went into this house; when the people around saw what happen, they were amazed and glorified God, Then Jesus saw a man named Matthew sitting at the receipt of custom Jesus said to him fellow me. He rose and fellow him, Jesus comes to make a difference and to show love and unity; the publicans and sinner came and sat with him and his disciples while they were eating their meal in the house; when the Pharisees saw this, they said unto Jesus disciples, why thy master eat with publican and sinners Jesus heard them he said unto them they that are whole need, not a physician only they that are sick, Jesus sends them to go and learn what those words mean Jesus told them I will have mercy and not sacrifice he did not come for the righteous but sinners to repentance then the disciple of John asking Jesus question about his disciple saying, why do the Pharisees and we fast but,

Thy disciple fasts, not Jesus answer them saying, can the children of the bride chamber mourn as long as the bride is with them. Still, the day will come when the bridegroom shall be taken away from them and then shall they fast, while Jesus was speaking, a certain man came to see Jesus because his daughter was dead he rose and fellow the Man with his disciple. Jesus was in a crowd, a woman with an issue of blood for years. She touches Jesus Garment. And instantly she was made whole that same hour when Jesus arrived at the house where the child was he said the maid his not dead Jesus put everyone out of the house and take her by the hand and raise her, and she was made hold from then it was spread abroad threw out all the land. Jesus departs two blind men fellow him crying Jesus thou son of David have mercy on us Jesus said to them believe ye that I can do this they say said unto him, yea Lord, Jesus touched their eyes, saying according to thy faith be it unto you. Their eyes were open again the fame went thru the country Jesus did many miracles and healing dumb speak blind eyes open devil was cast out Jesus went into the city and villages preaching the Gospel of the kingdom of heaven and healing every sickness and every disease among the people. Still, when Jesus saw the multitude, he was moved with compassion on them because they fainted and were scattered abroad as sheep having no shepherd Jesus turn to his disciple and said the harvest indeed his plenty, but the Laborers are few pray ye, therefore, the lord of the harvest that he will send labourer's into the harvest

Jesus Journey was very challenging; he faced many people trying to stop him from fulfilling his fathers will still never allow it to distract him on no farm for his relationship with his father. Jesus knows his destiny and his purpose for why he is coming to earth. As is children face testing as Jesus; we need to take on board all the example of Jesus and walk in the love and relationship with the Father as Jesus did; after he called all twelve disciples, he gave them power against the unclean spirit to cast them out and heal all manner of sickness and diseases.

Jesus twelve Disciples

These are the twelve disciples of Jesus who became apostles

Simon Peter and Andrew, his brother, James, the son of Zebedee and John his brother, Philip and Bartholomew Thomas and Matthew the publican James, the son of Alpheus whose surname was Thaddeus Simon the Canaanite and Judas Iscariot, who also betrayed Jesus he commanded them to go into the world and preach the gospel of the kingdom but not to go into the way of the Gentiles the city of the Samaritans but go to the last sheep of the house of Israel and preach the kingdom of heaven is at hand

And heal the sick cleanse the leopard raise the dead cast out devil freely you give freely you receive, Jesus being a good teacher prepared his disciple for the assignment ahead of them the same day Jesus went out of the house and gathered to gather unto him so that he went into a ship and sat down. The whole multitude stood on the shore, and he speaks many things unto them in parable saying behold a sower went forth to sow. The seed fell by the wayside the foul came and devoured it some fell among stony places they had not much earth and the sun-scorched them because they have no root they withered away some fell among thorns the thorns sprung up and choke them. Still, others fell on good ground and brought forth fruit some hundredfold, some sixtyfold some thirtyfold. Jesus spoke many parables about the kingdom of heaven. The disciple came and said unto him why speaks thou unto them in a parable, Jesus answer and said unto them because it is given unto you to know. Still, to them, it is not given after Jesus had finish speak these parables, he departed thence he came to his city and thought them in the synagogue insomuch they were astonished and said whence this man wisdom comes from and these mighty works hath done? Is he not the carpenter son? Are not this Mary son and his brother James and Josses and Simon and Judas? And his sister is they not all with us. Whence then hath this man. Is it not the same happening in our churches today?

The religious people today are still asking the same question when they saw those who desire to follow Jesus footstep has he fellow his father and the things he commands him to do while on earth this same world we are living in remember Jesus trial he was persecuted talk about and was despised and rejected by his very own yet they wickedness he heals the sick raise the dead feed the hungry and many more. He received no honour among his people. All religious leaders were having a form of godliness but denying the true power there off. They enjoy telling Jesus about the tradition of the elders and leaders. Jesus asks them, Why do ye transgress the commandment of God by your tradition. They never come to the reality of who they have among them. These people drew night with their mouths. They honored him with their lips, and their heart is far from him they worship, but it is only in vain. Their teaching of doctrine the commandment of men the Pharisees was offended after Jesus finished speaking the disciple came and said unto him knowing thou that the Pharisees were offended after they heard this saying Jesus answers and says, Every plant which my heavenly Father hath not planted shall be rooted up, their understanding was unfruitful they have no idea that he is the true King of Kings and Lord of all Lords the great creator he is, The master-builder, the only begotten son of the father, walking among them Jesus now question the disciple after feeding the great multitude, who do men say that I the Son of man am? Then answer them and said, some say that thou art John the Baptize some said Elias and others said Jeremiah or one of the prophets,

But Jesus said unto them. But who say ye that I am then Simon peter said thou art the Christ and the son of the living God then Jesus said to peter Blessed art thou Simon Bar-Jonah for flesh and blood hath not revealed it unto you but my Father which his in heaven. And I said unto thee thou art Peter, and upon this rock, I will build my church, and the gate of hell shall not prevail against it. And I will give you the *key to the kingdom of heaven, and whatsoever thou shall bind on earth be bind on earth shall be bound in heaven and whatsoever thou loosed in heaven. So the time comes that he began to tell his disciple how he must go unto Jerusalem, he suffered many things of the elders and chief priests and were killed and raised the third day again. Peter began to rebuke Jesus saying, be it far from the Lord this shall not be unto thee the same Peter whom God give the revelation of whom Jesus his but Jesus know it was not peter speaking that it was Satan, Jesus turns to Peter and rebukes the Spirit of Satan saying Get thee behind me Satan thou art an offence unto me for thou sourest not the things of God Jesus now speaks to his disciple. If any man comes after me, let him denied himself and take up the cross and follow me. Whosoever will save his life shall lose it, and whosoever will lose his life for my sake shall find it for what will a man profited if he shall gain the whole world and lose his one soul Or what shall a man give in exchange for his soul? For the son of man shall come in the glory of the father with the angel, and then he shall reward every man according to his works,*

Verily I say to you there be some standing here that shall not taste death till they see the son of men coming in his kingdom. Jesus speaks many parables unto his disciples about the kingdom of heaven; the Pharisees all so came and tempting him asking many questions.

When Jesus finished all he's saying, he departed from Galilee and to the coast of Judaea beyond Jordon great multitude fellow him Jesus heald

them all, The same his required of us as followers of Jesus Christ, study and understand our mission and stay focus so we can walk this partway the way we should, the scripture says thy word his a lamp unto my feet and a light to my part way it also says Jesus was tempted in all ways there is no temptation command, Among man that he was not drawn he's not asking us to do things that himself has not acquainted with, Jesus said I have overcome the world, in other words, if Jesus did it, so can we as his children. Let's make our life show forth the reflection of Jesus Christ in the earth for he lives in us; let's stay connected with the kingdom of God so we can influence men to the kingdom of heaven, we are his workmanship, and we are here to show forth his glory, Jesus taught the disciple how to live, in this present world we must be aware of certain kind of people the Pharisees were a challenging set of people the Pharisees and the counsel set out how they might entangle him in his talk. They sent out unto him their disciples with the Herodias, saying, master, we know that thou art true and teaches the way of God in truth is it lawful to give tribute to Caesar or not? Shall we give or shall we not,

But knowing their heart said, why tempt ye me ye hypocrites show me the tribute money *and bring unto him a penny. He said unto them whose is this image and superscription they said Caesar then said he unto them render therefore unto Caesar the things which are Caesar and unto God the things that are God. And it comes to pass when Jesus had finished all these saying he said unto his disciple know that after two days is the feast of the Passover and the son of men is betrayed to be crucified. So the chief priests and scribe and Elders of the people assembled unto the high priest place Caiaphas and consulted that they might take Jesus by subtlety and kill him, but they were afraid of the people making an uproar. So Jesus went to Bethany at Simon the leper house; a woman with an alabaster box of very precious ointment came and poured it on his head. As he sat at meat, the disciples were angry, saying to what purpose is this waste? For this, it Could have been sold for much and give to the poor. Jesus told then why troubles her for she has wrought a good work upon me Jesus let them now she hath poured this ointment my body she did it for my burial verily I said where ever this gospel shall be preached in the world there this woman that hath done this be told for a memorial of her. What she has done on the baby of Jesus*

This woman act of kindness was preparing Jesus for the other part of his Journey; some Journeys call for sacrifice and preparation, and Jesus is one of them,

Then one of his twelve disciples calls Judas Iscariot went unto the chief priests and said unto them, what will you give me, and I will deliver him into you. So they covenanted with him for thirty pieces of silver. And from that time he sought opportunity to betray Jesus, now it was time for Passover the feast of the unleavened bread the disciple came to Jesus to know where they would have it Jesus send them unto a certain man to said unto him that the Master said My time is at hand I will keep the Passover at his house with my disciple and the disciple did as Jesus appointed them and they made ready the Passover that evening he sat down with The twelve and brake bread and as they eat Jesus said verily I said unto you that one of you shall betray me and they were exceeding sorrowful and began every one of them to say unto him Lord is it I Lord, Jesus said he that dipped his hand with me in the dish the same shall betray me and Judas answer and said Master is it I he said thou then took the bread bless it and brake it they give the disciple saying take eat this is my body, and he takes the cup and gave thanks and gave it to them, Saying drink ye all of it, For this is my blood of the new Testament which is shed for the remission of sins and when they sang a hymn they went out into the mount of olive Jesus turn to his disciples and said all ye shall be offended because of me this night for it is written, I will smite the shepherd, and the sheep of the flock shall be scattered abroad. Still, after I have risen again, I will go before you into Galilee Peter answer and said unto Jesus. However, all men shall be offended because of thee,

Yet will I never be offended Jesus said to peter verily I said unto you that this night before the cock crow thou shall deny me thrice peter? So the disciples told Jesus that they will die with him. After which Jesus came with them into a place called Gethsemane and makes them sit while he went to pray; he took Peter and two sons of Zebedee and began to be sorrowful and very heavy, and said unto them my soul exceeding sorrowful even unto death tarry ye here and watch with me Jesus went a litter further, and fell on his face and prayed saying O my father if it is passable let this cup pass from me nevertheless not my will but as thou will, Then Jesus came unto his disciples and found them asleep and said unto peter could he not watch with me one hour, watch and pray Jesus said unto them that ye enter not into temptation the spirit indeed is willing. Still, the flesh his week then he went the second time and pray again that God will be done again he came to the disciple. So they were asleep the third time, went away and prayed the same word again. Then he came to them and said, sleep on and take your rest the hour his at hand and the son of man shall be betrayed into the hands of sinners.

JESUS WAS ARRESTED

Rise let us be going behold he is at hand that doth betray me while speaking Judas one of the twelve came and a great multitude with sword and from the chief priest and elders of the people Judas which betray Jesus give them a sign who so ever I kiss that he hold him fast then he came to Jesus and say hail master and kiss him Jesus said friend do what you came for, then they seize him and take him and arrested him; One of the disciples with Jesus took a sword and struck the slave of the high priest, and cut off his ear. So Jesus commands him to put up his sword, for all those who live fighting by the sword shall die by the sword.

Jesus trial

Jesus said unto him thus that I cannot appeal to my father, and he will immediately provide Me with more than twelve legions of angels? How then is the scripture fulfilled that it must happen this way? At that moment, Jesus said to the crowds have you come out with swords and clubs to arrest me like you would do with a robber every day? I used to sit in the porches and courts of the temple teaching, and you did not arrest me but. All this had taken place so that the scripture of the prophets would be fulfilled after he was arrested. The disciples deserted him and fled. Now Jesus was taken away to Caiaphas, the high priest where the scribe and the elders had gathered they were the Sanhedrin. Jewish high court, but Peter fellow him at a distance as far as the high priest's courtyard and went inside and sit with the guard to see the outcome. the whole council tried to get false witnesses to testify against Jesus so that they might have reason to put him to death; they find none even though many false witnesses came forward, then two came forward and testified. This man said I can tear down this temple of God and rebuild it in three days. The high priest stood up. He said to Jesus, have you no answer to give. What is it that these people are testifying against you? Still, Jesus kept silent, then the high prices said to Jesus, I call on you to swear a binding oath by the living God that you tell us whether you are the Christ the son of God, Jesus said to him you said it. Still, more than that, I tell you, Regardless of what you do with me now in the future, you will see me revealing as the son of men seated at the right hand of power and coming on the cloud of heaven? The high priest tore his robes exclaimed he had blasphemed by making himself God equal. We do not need any more evidence is a witness, we heard him blasphemy about the height price ask what do you think the answer he deserves to die. Jesus was spat on in the face; he was struck with the fist, and some slapped him, saying prophecy to us you Christ (Messiah Anointed) who was it that struck you.

The danger of a religious organization

Jesus came to earth not to establish a religion; he came to earth to return the Governmental system of the kingdom of heaven back to the territory in its rightful place and owner; let me break it down in st Matthew 4 v17 It said from the time Jesus began to preach and said, repent, this word means to change your mind, for the kingdom of heaven is at hand, Jesus was saying that the kingdom of heaven is with him, he has come to return it to its rightful place, Mankind was sent to earth to influence the earth realm which is the visible realm the heavenly kingdom the unseen realm, Adam lost this domain by handing it over to the serpent the devil, in the garden of Eden, this domain was the kingdom of heaven. All his access to heaven resource and the commonwealth is common because it's for all; Adam lost the protection of the kingdom, for he was no longer under the law of the kingdom. Therefore, he was no longer governed by the kingdom of heaven. Every king glory is to take care of their territory as long as they colonies it for the colony is wealthy as the kingdom, So is the function of the kingdom of heaven King Jesus our father God takes pleasure in caring for is creation on earth, that's the reason why Adam lose the kingdom and all its resources for he was given everything that was in heaven on earth and we all were in Adams loin when it was given to him; therefore, it was also given to us when the fall the world plunge into the realm of darkness, where satin ravish everything to his evil content Religion comes about after the fall of men; things reverse God used to go and seek Adam in the cool of the day Adam never had a hymn book to sing so that God would go and see him he never had a pulpit and a P, A system, the man and his wife were naked, and they were not ashamed, now its man seeking God, so man needs a choir to sing in the presence of God, and if you do not dress with a particular dress code you are not seen as being holy, there is also implemented a specific way and day to worship all this happen after the fall, the children of Israel had to govern by-the laws because they were doing abominable things among themself,

 This brings me to my point the Jewish people were religious people they could not come to term with Jesus teaching about the kingdom of heaven and the love of his father, and telling them they should love their neighbour as themself it was a command thing to stone and kill someone if they break the law Jesus told them to give to those who don't have this also was strange it was the law to take away property as payment and enslave their children as a bondman, and the list goes on, keeping the law of Moses was more important than the true gospel, these are the things that suppurate Jesus teaching from others, that the reason he *answers the Sanhedrin Jewish High Court,*

The only thing they were short of was the truth. Poilat confers that he did not know it. So he asks Jesus what his truth? Not their question it was pure religious talk, and he never gets involved with a religious conversation for he is a king and a king only reply to kingdom talk, so when Jesus was taken to pilot the Roman Governor, he answered when it was necessary to you may ask why the Romans are not religious people they are kingdom empire, they speak the language of the kingdom, the same language as Jesus. So we should take a leaf from Jesus book, do not get into a foolish and unprofitable debate with religious people. You will end up like peter denied Jesus just to compromise and please the wrong set of people.

Peter denied Jesus

Now Pete was sitting outside warming himself by the fire in the courtyard with the crowd that shout crucified him; then a servant girl came to Peter and said, you too were with Jesus the Galilean. But Peter denied it before them all, saying I do not know what you are talking about again. Two more times, Peter was asked. For the third times, he demised peter swear then the rooster crow peter remember what Jesus told him you will deny me three times then he went away and wept bitterly in repentance,

When it was morning, all the chief priest and the elders of the people (Sanhedrin, Jewish High Court) conferred together against Jesus how to put him to death under the roman rules, they have no power to execute anyone, so they bound him and led him away hand him over to palate the governor of Judea. Then latter has the authority to condemn prisoners to death. Judas had betrayed Jesus, but when he learned that

The death sentence

Jesus had been sentenced to death; he was sorry for what he had done; he returned the 30 silver coins to the chief priest and leaders and said I have sinned by betraying a man who has never done anything wrong, so what? That's your problem, they reply. So Judas threw the money into the temple and then went out and hanged himself; the chief price picked up the money and said this money was paid to have a man killed we cannot put it in the temple treasury; then they had a meeting and decided to buy a field that belonged to someone who made clay pot they wanted to use it as a graveyard for foreigners this is why people call that place field of blood.

The word of the prophet Jeremiah came to pass early next morning; all the chief priests and the nation's leader met and decided that Jesus should be put to death; they tied him up and led him away to pilot Jesus was brought before pilot the governor who asked him are you the king of the Jews those are your word Jesus answer

When the chief priest and leader brought their charges against him, he did not say a thing Pilot asked him, Don't you hear what crime they say you have committed? But Jesus did not say anything, and the governor was incredibly amazed. Passover, the Governor, always freed a prisoner chosen by the people at that time, a well-known terrorist Named. Barabbas was in jail, so when the crowd came together, Pilate asked them which prisoner they want me to set free. Do you want Barabbas or Jesus, who is called the Messiah?

Pilate knows the leader had brought Jesus to him because they were Jealous; while pilots judging the case, his wife sends him a Message it said don't have anything to do with that innocent man I have Nightmares because of him but the chief priest and leaders Convinced the crowd to ask for Barabbas to be set free and for Jesus to kill Pilate asked the crowd again Which of these two men do you want me to set free Barabbas they shouted, Pilate asked them, what am I to do with Jesus who is called the Messiah they all yelled Nail him to a cross, Pilate saw that there was nothing he could do and that the people were starting to riot. So Pilate took water and washes his hands in front of them and said I won't have anything to do with killing this man; you are the one doing it, everyone answers our families, and we will take the blame for his death, and Pilate set Barabbas free then he ordered the soldiers to beat Jesus with a whip and nail to a cross.

The Governor Soldiers led Jesus into the fortress and brought together the rest of the troop and Jesus clothes and put a scarlet robe on him; they make a crown out of thorn *branches and place it on his head, and they put a stick in his right hand. The soldiers knelt and pretended to worship him; they make fun of him and shouted, hey, you king of the Jews. They took the stick from him and beat him on the head when these soldier's finished making fun of Jesus; they took off the robe they put his clothes back on him and led him off to nail him to the cross. On the way, they meet a man named Simon, who was from Cyrene, and they forced him to carry Jesus cross. They came to a place name Golgotha which means the place of a Skull; there, they give Jesus some wine mixed with a drug to ease the pain, but when Jesus tasted what it was, he refuses to drink it. The soldiers nailed Jesus to the cross and gambled to see who would get his clothes, and then they sat down to guard him. Above his head, they put a sign that told why he was nailed to the cross; it read this is JESUS the KING of the JEWS. The soldiers also nailed two criminal on crosses, one on the right of Jesus and the other on this left. People who pass by said terrible things about Jesus; they shook their head and shouted, so you are the one who claimed you could tear down the temple and build it again in three days if you are Godson save yourself and come down from the cross. The chief priest and leaders, also the teachers of the law of Moses, all make fun of Jesus; they said he saved others, but he can't save himself if he is the king of Israel should come down from the cross,*

Then we will believe him. Moses trusted God, so let God save him if he wants to. He even said he was Godson.

One of the criminals also said cruel things to Jesus, but the other finds forgiveness by asking him to remember him. At noon the sky turned dark and stayed that way until three O clock; then, about that time, Jesse shouted, Eli Eli, Sachthani, which mean my God, why have you deserted me? Some of the people there heard Jesus and said he called for Elijah; one of them at once ran and grabbed a sponge; he soaked it in wine, then put it on a stick and held it up to Jesus. Others said, wait, and let's see if Elijah will come and save him; once again, Jesus shouted and then he died. Then, at once, the curtain in the temple was torn in two from the top to the bottom; the earth shook, and the rock split apart; Graves opened, and many of God people were raised from death to life they went into the holy city where they were seen by many people. The officer and the soldiers guarding Jesus felt the earthquake and saw everything else that happened; they were frightened and said this man was God, Son, many women had come with Jesus from Galilee to be of help to him, and they were there looking on at a distance Mary Magdalene Mary the mother of James and Joseph and the mother of James and John and some of the women. That evening a wealthy disciple named Joseph from the town of Arimathea went and asked for Jesus body. Pilate gives the order for it to be given to Joseph, who took the body and wrapped it in clean linen then Joseph put the body in his tomb that has been cut from solid rock and has never been used;

He rolled a big stone against the entrance to the tomb and went away. All this time, Mary Magdalene and the other Mary were away sitting across from the grave. On the next day, the Sabbath,

Jesus is Risen

They said, Sir, we remember what this liar said while he was still alive. He claimed that he would come back from the dead on the third days, so please order the tomb to be carefully guarded for three days the fair Jesus disciples may go and steal his body. After that, they will tell the people he has been raised to live. This last lie will be worse than the first one Pilate said to them All right, take some of your soldiers and guard the tomb as well as you know, so they sealed it tight and place soldiers at the entrance making sure his disciple did not come and steal the body by night; therefore, they guard it, the Sabbath was over, and it was almost daybreak on Sunday when Mary Magdalene and the other Mary went to see the tomb. Suddenly a strong earthquake struck, and the angel came down from heaven; he rolled away from the stone and sat on it; the angel look as bright as lightning, and his clothes were white as snow the guard shook from fear and fell as though they were dead the angel said to the woman don't be afraid I know you are looking for Jesus who was nail to a cross he isn't here, God has raised him to life just as Jesus said he would come to see the place where his body lies Now hurry to tell his disciples he has been raised to life is on his way to Galilee go there. You will see him; this is what I came to tell you the women were frightened and yet very happy have they hurry from the tomb and run to tell his disciple.

Suddenly, he met them and greeted them; they went near him, held on to his feet, and worshipped him. Jesus said, don't be afraid tell my follower to go to Galilee they will see me there;

Tell the truth

While the women on their way, some soldiers who had been guarding the tomb went into the city; they told the chief priests everything that had happened, so the chief priest met with the leaders and decided to bribe the soldiers with a lot of Money. They said to the soldiers tell everyone that Jesus disciple came during the night and stole his body while they were asleep, If the Governor hears about this, we will talk to him you won't have anything to worry about the soldiers took the money and did what we're told the people of Judea still tell each other the story, but Jesus did appear to his disciple on many occasion

What story are you telling today? Are we tell the true story of Jesus, how he gave his life for us he bears the shame and takes those beating for us they hung him high on that wooden cross using nails in his hands and feet and parse him in his side blood and water come gushing down Oh what pain he went true for this hold world even then men still refuse Jesus. Still, he bids us tell them just the same even if they don't believe then there is a day coming when every man will give an account of what they hear of the Lord Jesus and how they respond to is word let no man pay you to reject Jesus, They did it then and still doing it today.

Do not be weight in a balanced and found

wanting let your light shine where ever you are even it may be you are the only one that makes the difference you are unique and special, so was Jesus he too was special to mankind he gave his life as a ransom for us. He journeys from heaven to earth to show us the way back home to the father and restore us to our original state. No way being religious could have given this new life again. Today, people are still searching for this truth, and it is there before their very eyes, the Jewish priest and rabies knew who he was. However, they still denied him. Let's not crucified him again by living a separate life from the one he died to give us a new and happy life, a life filled with hope, tell the world about his love for us and live a life of truth.

I NOW YOU ARE BLESS

www.ingramcontent.com/pod-product-compliance
Lightning Source LLC
Chambersburg PA
CBHW071501070526
44578CB00001B/410